How to Heal Stress, Anxiety, and Fear.

Releasing Trauma in Easy Steps.

By Juliet Yelverton

Preface

This Book is for You If…

If you have experienced three or more of the following things:

☐ Fear

☐ Anxiety

☐ Stress

☐ Depression

☐ Rage

☐ Shame

☐ Despair

☐ Accident of any kind

☐ Loss of loved one

☐ Loss of home

☐ Loss of job

☐ Loss of identity

☐ Loss of freedom

☐ Abuse of any kind - physical, emotional, sexual, spiritual

☐ Acrimonious break up of a relationship

☐ Attack

☐ Bullying

☐ Surgery

☐ Life-threatening illness

☐ From a family in which there is addiction/alcoholism

☐ From a family with stressed and overworking parents

☐ From a family with rigid fundamental belief systems

☐ From a family with members in prison

☐ From a family where parents were divorced

☐ Did you suffer poverty?

☐ Were you a refugee?

☐ Did you live in a war zone?

How did you do with these questions?

If you feel that you have experienced three or more of these conditions, you will find a lot of helpful information here as well as the means to, step by step, change the conditions of your life and heal your trauma.

CONTENTS

CONTENTS

INTRODUCTION

What you need to understand about trauma.

"I don't have any trauma," was my instant response to Juliet's suggestion that I experience a trauma healing session. And I now realise that ego resistance is the biggest challenge to opening to trauma healing. You literally have to be prepared to take off your safe coat of armour and become vulnerable, to go deep into what lies beneath repeating life patterns."

Rachel Elnaugh

Has it happened to you?

Have you experienced a high level of stress and anxiety? Have you had an accident or a loss? Do you feel depressed and under-motivated? Did you have an apparently happy childhood but have feelings of distress that doesn't seem to tie up with this? Are you suffering from addiction of any kind? Or maybe you have physical ailments that don't seem to get better such as auto-immune disease of some kind? Or maybe digestive problems, or high blood pressure, maybe difficulty sleeping? These are just a very few of the types of conditions that can indicate that you are suffering from trauma.

But what is trauma?

Once you understand that the word trauma refers to the impact in your nervous system, you will be able to heal it.

Trauma is not the bad event that has happened sometime in your past, it is what is happening to you now, today, and every day of your life, because of the impact of a past bad event on your nervous system.

The experience of trauma is felt when your autonomic nervous system becomes stuck in a dis-regulation causing you to have symptoms that make your life uncomfortable and often downright miserable. This can happen as a result of a single past event, or a whole series of small events that gradually eroded your feelings of safety and well-being. This may have happened slowly over a long period of time.

My intention in writing this book is to bring you an easily accessible way to significantly improve your life. Without fully realising it, you may be suffering the often-devastating effects of trauma. The good news is that it can be healed safely using the simple methods that I will describe to you here. It may take time and perseverance, but you can heal and your life can be free from anxiety, depression, anger, and many of the other nervous system manifestations of trauma running in your system. Trauma is a dis-regulation of the nervous system. Your nervous system can be reset to normal functioning using the methods that I will describe here.

Many people, just like you, have healed trauma using these powerful and well-tried healing methods.

However, if you have a high degree of trauma, complex trauma, or developmental trauma, you are advised to seek out an experienced therapist who can work with you using a somatic (body-based) approach. There is more information about what can help you at the end of the book, as well as lots of help along the way. This kind of trauma occurs as a result of bad things happening to you as a baby or young child which disrupted your safe relationship and attachment with your Mother or other primary carer.

Will healing my trauma cause me to feel overwhelmed and bring up lots of unpleasant memories?

The process of healing your trauma may bring up information that will need to be processed. It is important that you have some support in your life and you are well resourced when you do this work. The aim of this book is to teach you about resourcing and to encourage you to build a supportive network for yourself of friends and family.

It is however a misconception that you have to stir up lots of past memories to heal trauma. The combination of resourcing, somatic experiencing and activities that utilise a mind/body interaction such as dancing or yoga are very effective when used together to heal trauma. So do not be afraid to start healing now. You do not have to dig around in your memories and churn through your past life in order to heal. In fact this can be counter productive and even re-traumatising.

It may happen that memories <u>do</u> come up as you start to heal and as you begin to re-evaluate your life. It's important here, not to plunge into lots of intense feelings but to pace yourself with resourcing.

It may be that you want a sense of resolution with past events, so you may wish to revisit memories. If you do, then do it in a <u>light</u> way. Notice what memories are coming up and how they make you feel, but don't stay with them. Once you notice them, then take the time to go and do something different that takes you away from feeling too intensely into these past events and consequent emotions.

Imagine the events that you are experiencing as if you were seeing them on a cinema screen that you can distance yourself from.

To heal trauma and to reset the nervous system you **need to establish a sense of well-being and safety in your body and your life** so that your nervous system can stop panicking. The problem is when you are traumatised, that your brain cannot differentiate between something that happened in the past and something in the present moment. When you stir up lots of memories, your brain makes a mistake and believes those things are happening now in this moment. You will then get taken into a high level of activation which will bring intense feelings. This is because your brain and nervous system mistakenly interprets that you are in a life threatening situation and is doing what it needs to do to protect you. I will explain about that later. For the moment, it suffices to know that the best thing that you can be doing is to resource and to give distance to intense feelings so that you can reassure your brain and nervous system that you are **NOT** in a life-threatening situation anymore.

REMEMBER - the first step in healing trauma is to create a sense of safety in your body.

Before I go on to talk in-depth about trauma, let me share a little about myself and my experience in life that has made me deeply knowledgeable about trauma. This has enabled me to develop the skills and compassion to be able to help you in this way.

And if you want to begin working now, in a guided way, scan the QR code above and you can check out my 'How To Heal Your Trauma' Online Programme"

CHAPTER 1

My Personal Experiences with Trauma:

I was born just post-war, which, as you can imagine, was a time when there was a lot of shock and trauma affecting the general population as a result of the horrors of the war.

Being of a poor mining family, poverty was also an issue. My early childhood was smitten by many after-effects of the disaster of war. I often lacked adequate care and protection. We were very poor, money was scarce and resources were thin, I suffered much emotional anguish as a result.

My parents were very young and not able to provide appropriate care for me. They themselves were struggling having grown up in the war which was terribly traumatic for them.

I know from personal birth research, using the same methods that I now use with my clients, that my time in the womb was also beset with difficulties. Poverty and war always cause extreme distress and trauma, and typically there was continual conflict in my family.

Not surprising since my father was one of 16 children in a poor mining family and my teenage parents had to make their home in the living room of the two-up two-down little house which had the toilet at the end of the garden. Very sadly, my parents were divorced by the time I was about a year old.

They had no emotional support or help from anyone and were not able to cope with the intensity of the unconscious and unresolved trauma in their own nervous systems. They were struggling to make the best sense of it that they could, but it was beyond their understanding and capability. They were at a loss as to how to take care of me, especially when my mother then had another baby and had two to look after.

There was not a proper secure home for me anywhere, and in their attempts to deal with their feelings of overwhelm, I was then passed from relative to relative to be taken care of. This led to me being unable to bond with any particular person, and I did not manage to put down roots, leading to a great deal of insecurity, poor self-esteem, and a sense that I didn't matter to anyone.

Human beings need to bond and feel part of a family so this experience was possibly one of the most traumatising and damaging that could happen to me. In particular, babies and tiny children need to feel safe and secure with one carer, since their very life and survival depends upon that person. It caused me to have a traumatic wound known as 'attachment damage', which took me many years to heal.

As a teenager in a 'broken home', it was hard to feel any sense of security or purpose; I had to make do the best I could and was often vulnerable to the abuse of other similarly unfortunate people who had suffered in their childhood. My education also suffered dramatically; I changed schools about 20 times. I was an intelligent and creative person, but there was no-one in my life able to reflect that back to me. Instead, I lacked intellectual stimulation and was continually bullied because I was always the 'new girl' in school.

Consequently, I made some bad relationship choices and, over the first 40 years of my life, I was married in turn to three different partners each with their own traumatic patterns including alcoholism and serious addictions. They were unable to be emotionally available to me. This stirred up deep feelings or pain and abandonment and I felt very lonely. It was like a repeat of what had happened to me as a small child.

Does this sound familiar to you? Being in those relationships was very distressing for me; I felt trapped. I did not know how to move into a better situation. In fact, there was a period when I thought that I was crazy because everything that I knew to be good and right was turned upside down. Living with addictive partners, or being in a family with addictive parents, is very traumatising. How many of us make bad choices in life because we have been so wounded and possibly have had parents with addictions?

During this time, I also suffered much loss through the suicide of my brother and then the death of my first two babies. When my marriage broke up my baby which was then my third child and first one that had survived after birth, was taken from me. Despite going through the court system, I could not have easy access to him. I now know that this is an ordeal that face many mothers in the break up of traumatic relationships, through no fault of their own. The court and social care systems are not trauma informed and often cause more suffering and trauma in families which are already traumatised. This is an example of where we as a society need to overhaul our social system to become more supportive, caring and trauma integrated.

In total I gave birth to six children, two died; four survived. Each one of them was born prematurely and was in an incubator for the first month of their lives. It was a terrifying and very distressing time for me. With time and reflection I can now see how this painful experience taught me how to take care of very fragile babies, to nurture them and help them grow strong. I learned much patience and endurance during this time even though my heart was breaking over about a ten year period because of the loss that I had been through, and the fear that my babies would die.

Finally, in my forties, I moved to France. I had felt that finally I had healed, met my dream partner and was embarking on a whole new life. I had given birth to two beautiful baby daughters and I felt that finally I could be happy. We had bought a beautiful rural farmhouse where we could be self sufficient and live in peace and abundance. It was not to be. The cards seemed to be stacked against us as we stepped into another emotional maelstrom. The joint trauma patterns between myself and my new husband collided with the collective unresolved trauma of world war two.

The journey to France set off to a bad start as we were hit from behind by an articulated truck, narrowly avoiding the head of my sleeping baby in the back of our van. The van was a 'right off' mechanically but we managed to limp to the destination of the area where we were searching for a dream home. It was the first of three serious accidents that I had over a period of about five years. Again the theme of trauma repeating itself!

The shock and severity of the accidents however, paled in significance alongside the experiences that were to follow the final move into our new rural paradise. Unknown to us at the time, this part of France had also been badly affected by the war and the whole community had suffered as a result of a Nazi massacre. A monument in the village told of the brutal attack on 6th August 1945, but not speaking French at the time we did not understand what it was written there. It seems now that I think about it that a psychic scar was left on the landscape from the horrific events that took place in the small hamlet and in the valley, including the shooting of the father of the house that we were buying, on that day of the massacre.

What soon become apparent however was that we had unwittingly bought a house in a valley dominated by fascism and with both the police and the mayor in collusion with, in some way which we could never get to the bottom of, the two people who had been squatting in the house that we had just bought. None of this was explained to us by the estate agent. We bought the house and stepped into a hell when the two people had to be forcibly removed. They moved to the next house and started a campaign of terror against us which we endured for 8 years. I could write books about this if I ever find the time!

This couple were emotionally unhinged, psychotic, psychopathic 'national front' supporters. They were used to having things their own way. They attacked us from the very first and when we came to move into our house we found that they had gutted it of all the utilities, electricity and plumbing and destroyed our spring water supply. They then proceeded to spread malicious rumours about us as well as physically attack us, kill our animals, repeatedly call the police on us, steal parcels of our land and have the mayor harass us.

These experiences overwhelmed my already damaged nervous system and I was continually on 'active alert', expecting an attack at any time. It seriously undermined my physical health.

Throughout this whole period, I had to deal not only with the pain of these situations, but also help my four children come through the frightening experiences in a way that would enable them to be happy and functional human beings. Despite doing the best I could, my children have still been themselves marked by trauma. Highly traumatised parents give birth to babies with cortisol levels less equipped to deal with stress and more prone to traumatisation. Fortunately, my children have much more insight into what is happening to them than I did as a teenager, so are healing much quicker than was possible for me. Unfortunately the pain and stress was more than our fragile family could endure and my marriage broke up and I returned to England with our children.

Many years later, my final traumatic experience was becoming seriously ill with a heart infection as a result of all the stress that I had been through. I spent two months in hospital and was advised that I needed heart surgery. I managed to heal myself through this intense episode and am entirely well now. This gave me further insight into how being in hospital and having medical interventions can be seriously traumatising.

Anything that happens to our bodies, such as drug therapy or surgery, is registered by the body as being 'life-threatening' even though the intention of the medical establishment is to help you to heal. Because they do not have an understanding of the trauma that they are inducing, and only looking at the physical body, they are unaware of the harm that comes with medical treatments.

This is another social area where we need to bring trauma informed and trauma integrated treatments. We are not just isolated physical bodies. We are complex social beings that have bodies that are interconnected with emotional, mental and spiritual responses.

I was very distressed in hospital watching what the other patients were going through, as well as experiencing the treatments that I was receiving. It was a hellish experience and I didn't feel that the hospital was a place where one could receive the care that was necessary for profound healing. It was a time of much observation and reflection of what was going on around me and what I was subjected to. My friends supported me enormously emotionally and brought good quality food and supplements.

This very intense and emotionally demanding experience challenged me to bring everything that I knew about health and healing into action to support my recovery. I knew that I had to work on spiritual, emotional and mental levels to recover. When I finally left the hospital, it was without having the open heart surgery to replace the valve that they had told me was badly damaged by the infection. That was over a decade ago and I have never been ill with a heart problem or any symptoms of a failing heart. I live a physically active life and am a lot fitter than many people much younger than myself. We are remarkable beings and have full capacity to heal so give yourself the opportunity to do so, even if you feel that it is not possible.

My life has been one intensely traumatic experience after another, and it might have been that I ended up like many of the unfortunate souls that I met along the way whose lives had fallen apart, or had committed suicide, or become an addict. All of these have been people in my life, which in itself is very distressing.

However, I did not intend this to happen to me, and I feel that at a soul level it was all meant to be. It has enabled me to become deeply knowledgeable about the 'terrain' of trauma. What I had been through had caused me to be nervous, anxious, often depressed, and at times also feeling suicidal. From early childhood, my body would shake when I got distressed, and after the car accidents, I developed the symptoms of post-traumatic stress disorder. I have now healed myself of all these symptoms except for a slight tremble to my hands when I am under pressure. I can also say without hesitation that I am a very happy and active person with a dynamic vision of what I want to dedicate my life to.

Despite the difficult circumstances of my life, I was determined to make it successful and to empower myself to move out of the challenges of my family background. In the mid '70s I studied for a Science Degree, and in the early '80s, a Master's Degree. I was the first member of my family to attain any kind of education since the norm was to leave school at fifteen and to get a job in a factory.

Even with this education, my health was still suffering, so, in the early '90s, I undertook the first of a series of trainings that progressively qualified me to work with trauma. Firstly, I trained with Franklyn Sills, at the Karuna Institute in Devon, in Cranio-Sacral Therapy and a foundation in Core Process Psychotherapy. I then did all the advanced Cranio sacral course that were available. I also trained with Babette Rothschild in trauma resolution and Mike Boxhall in the spiritual dimensions of healing.

Later, I trained with Karlton Terry in Pre- and Peri-natal Trauma Resolution and also Understanding Baby's Body Language, (through which they are able to share the traumatic experiences that happened to them in utero). I have also read, researched, and worked with a large number of clients. I latter trained with Thomas Hubl in Collective Trauma resolution and Dr. Pat Ogden online in Sensorimotor Psychotherapy at an introductory level. This is an integrative approach to healing trauma that is very helpful for complex developmental trauma.

Prior to these trainings, I had also studied herbalism, homeopathy, and kinesiology and naturopathy at a basic level, but fully embraced life as a therapist in 1992. By 2001, my therapy business began to be focussed particularly on healing trauma, and in 2005 I established Healing Waters Sanctuary as a 'safe retreat space' where people could either just come and relax, or get the help to heal their trauma.

In 2007 I also established the Healing Gardens Cooperative, where people in the local community can heal their bodies and create good health through gardening and eating fresh organic produce. A healthy diet is an essential part of healing the body and emotions.

In 1992 I had bought a property in France which I described earlier where despite the difficulties and harassment we had managed to be self sufficient in fruit, vegetables and dairy products through the care of a herd of goats.

In 2001 I returned to the UK because of the problems that happened there. Following my return to the UK there were 2 major fires on the property, In the first fire, the huge beautiful barn that I had hoped to renovate and run groups in was gutted by fire. The following year the end of the main house was burnt.

On reflection, these fires in themselves may represent traumatic recapitulation or recycling. The original trauma of the Nazi Massacre had involved a hotel being set on fire and burnt to the ground. I was devastated by the fires and not having any money at the time had no idea what to do, especially since there was no insurance on the barn. Several years later, a solution presented itself and I found a way to buy out my ex-husband who was still living there in a similar hopelessly stuck situation.

Little by little I managed to pull all the devastation together and meanwhile, just as I had visualised on so many occasions earlier, the abusive people who had terrorised us, also had a marital split and sold their property. Happiness returned to the valley in the moving in of some really beautiful, loving kind neighbours.

In 2012, I finally began rebuilding the barn perhaps with the aim of running trauma healing retreats and workshops. The nature is so profound in the valley and it is a natural place of healing. It is surrounded by forest and full of wild life and has a deep tranquility that gently caresses the soul. Following all these difficult and painful experiences there has been a lot of healing in my family. When one person decides to heal, it affects everyone because as you heal, you begin to relate differently. Healing is all about your relationships. We cannot heal in isolation.

Apart from my personal experiences of trauma I have travelled extensively to many parts of the world where there is ongoing suffering through famine, war, and poverty. I have worked in a Mother Theresa Orphanage in India, and I have also been involved with Famine Relief work in Eritrea in the Horn of Africa.

REMEMBER - that even if you have had a lot of difficult experiences, you can heal, just like I did..

In my therapy work, I have now witnessed almost every imaginable kind of distress that can happen to a human being. Relationship issues and abuse is often high on the list and often involves many members of families. Both the people who are abused, and their abusers, suffer terribly.

I would also add that there is not a person on the planet that is perpetrating abuse who has not themselves been abused. Compassion is a vital part to healing trauma since, by its nature, it creates an endless spiral of suffering, and is contagious in that it causes a recapitulation of the original circumstances in an attempt for the traumatised soul to heal.

If you are a person working with other people who are traumatised, or you are in the caring services, it is likely that you yourself will get traumatised. Trauma is contagious in that it undermines your ability to self regulate when in relationship to other disturbed and traumatised people. When working in this capacity, it is wise to take care and to take lots of time for resourcing away from the stress of these relationships.

Through my deep experience and understanding of trauma, I am committed to bringing freedom from violence and abuse to each individual on the planet. I pledge to bring relief of fear engendered by trauma. I aim to eradicate the needless recycling of trauma and, in doing so, there will be an end to war and all the evils associated with it. I may not see this happen in my lifetime but I am committed to doing whatever is in my power to bring a significant shift in the understanding of trauma and how it underpins all the other suffering.

I am passionate to teach and heal everyone in a profoundly safe way, and bring an end to suffering. I may not achieve this lofty goal on my own but I am setting in motion, having learnt from my own experiences and studied with other trauma experts, a shift to a more trauma informed and trauma integrated world. If you like this is a vow that may take me lifetimes to achieve. I have a buddhist leaning and after so many experiences I have a sense that we are so much more than our physical bodies and that we have infinite lives.

My current means of doing this work is by healing from pre- and peri-natal trauma through my Healing Birth Wounds Workshops, together with Julia Duthie, midwife and pre-birth educator. The trauma that happens in these stages of human development is at the root of all other trauma experienced later in life. I am also running a Professional Trauma Skills Training for Therapists, enabling them both to clear their own trauma and to be able to facilitate their clients in a deeper, more conscious and healing manner. I also offer an advanced level of training to build a Sangha (or association) of Emissaries to bring Trauma Informed Consultancy to our Social Sectors and Corporate Management.

I highly recommend that if you are suffering from trauma, you seek professional help alongside the self-help that you find in this book and other 'Healing Trauma' materials that I make available. Besides this, there is a growing wave of trauma informed people and there is a lot of information available. But be aware, healing is a deep process and involves working through the body. It is not just a mental process or just an emotional process.

Many people say that they are 'trauma informed' or 'trauma healers' and it is also a 'buzzword' or the 'in-thing'. Trauma is a physical problem in the body and healing involves working with the body. The true signs of healing are to be seen when you witness that your life is changing and becoming more functional and that you are able to regulate your nervous system and emotions in times of difficulty and stress so that you do not get overwhelmed and spin out of control.

As you heal, your relationships will also heal. Many people mistake having a very intense emotional experience, stimulated by a healing technique, as a sign of healing. This is not so. Intense experiences can bring much to the surface which in itself can become overwhelming and potentially re-traumatising unless well integrated emotionally and psychologically with the help of good therapeutic support founded in a safe and trusted relationship.

UNDERSTANDING TRAUMA

What are the situations that create trauma?

Trauma is caused when the nervous system is overwhelmed and over activated and does not return back to a pre-activation level. This can be the result of numerous circumstances. A person can experience a very overwhelming situation but is not necessarily traumatised if they are well resourced at the time. Basically, trauma happens when a person experiences something that is life-threatening or feels as if it is life-threatening. Or if they witness someone else go through a life-threatening event.

It can also happen over a period of time with smaller events, such as ongoing neglect or ongoing emotional anguish, that gradually create a feeling of helplessness and erodes the person's sense of 'selfhood'. Trauma can even happen in families where children believe that they are 'happy' and 'well cared for'. Although externally and materially family life appears to be good, if the fundamental core needs of the child are not met, then traumatisation can occur. It is later in life, when that person begins to experience emotional and physical problems, that they discover as part of their healing journey that beneath the veneer of a happy family, their true needs were not taken care of.

What types of events lead to trauma?

- Physical violence or the threat of physical violence.
- Serious accidents or attacks such as might happen in a war.
- Transport accidents or industrial accidents.
- Severe illness or long-term illness.
- Medical treatments, interventions, and surgery.
- Birth interventions of any kind are traumatic for both mother and baby and often the father as well.
- Emotional and psychological abuse.
- Loss and bereavement.
- Being a member of a dysfunctional family.
- Living with a partner or parents that are suffering from alcoholism or addiction.

People working in the caring professions are also liable to become traumatised. People such as police or fire brigade officers, doctors or nurses, or even psychotherapists and trauma resolution therapists. It is the witnessing of the trauma or even the retelling of it that can overwhelm the nervous system of the witnessing person. Traumatised people are said to 'exude' peptides, known as 'extracorporeal peptides' into the atmosphere. This is one of the ways that a therapist can become traumatised because they absorb the peptides. Do you know what it feels like when someone near you suddenly becomes activated into fear or anger? It causes your activation levels to leap dramatically, especially if you have trauma in your own system. You then also get angry or fearful.

Can our prenatal lives be traumatic?

There is a large body of research into our pre-natal development, through regression of individuals into their personal experiences. This research has been conducted by pre birth psychologists and educators such as Dr William Emerson, Frank Lake and Carlton Terry. Thousands of anecdotal experiences have been documented with a surprising correspondence between the accounts.

It has been discovered that all phases of prenatal development are potentially traumatic since each stage of transition from pre-conception to birth is life-threatening for the egg, sperm and blastocyst, (the small organism that you once were immediately after conception). For instance, very few of the millions of sperm and thousands of eggs end up surviving, they all face death along the way on their journey towards conception. It is unlikely that the sperm or egg will survive through to conception or that the blastocyst will make it to implantation. If implantation of the blastocyst is successful, then the resulting embryo then has to be able to survive into becoming a foetus. If the tiny foetus survives thus far and develops into a baby, it is still vulnerable to any number of shocks in the womb. Babies growing in the womb of a mother who is in an abusive relationship will become traumatised as her stress hormones will, in turn, cause the baby to be stressed. They will also lower the resilience of that child to stress later in life, and even predispose the child to addiction.

These early pre and post conception stages are rarely considered as being subject to trauma by conventional medical and midwifery. But many see that birth can hold many dangers both for Mother and Baby. One reason for this is that all stages of birth are traumatic because the average size head of a baby is often larger than the pelvis of the mother. Even though the bones of the head are soft and flexible it is still a very traumatic event. Pre and perinatal (before and after birth) trauma are something that we are all afflicted with. This creates an imprint or blueprint for later trauma in life. This is a result of something called recapitulation, in which the psyche of the person who has been traumatised brings forth other situations of a similar nature in order to become conscious of the original event as a means to eventually heal it. Traumatic recapitulation is the cause of those patterns in our lives that keep repeating endlessly, continually causing distress until consciousness develops around the cause of the pattern and therapy is done that heals it. Dr. Peter Levine says that traumatic recapitulation is the cause of the greatest suffering in the world.

Having described how potentially traumatic our pre and peri natal lives can be, let me re-assure you that it is possible to be conceived and be born with less trauma if there is conscious awareness around the process. Planning for conception and being pregnant in a happy supportive environment and giving birth peacefully and naturally will make an enormous difference in this.

Returning to the theme of traumatic recapitulation, you may have experienced distressing events of the same nature that keep repeating themselves throughout your life. Do you have an awareness of that happening to you? I myself had three very similar car accidents within a short sequence of time. I have also had several other difficult and painful themes in my life around relationships and childbirth that have repeated. It made me feel despairing and in shock that the same thing was happening over and over. There may be patterns in your life that seem to senselessly repeat which may have had their roots in one of those prenatal stages when you almost died. Patterns can also repeat down the ancestral line. Sometimes a generation may be missed. This can even happen on a collective level with entire populations. It is important to discover the links of your own trauma story and of the culture that you live within.

Trauma is endlessly repetitive and is passed down the generations until it is healed. It is for this reason that I am so passionate about bringing awareness about trauma. Once we have had one traumatising experience, our nervous system is more prone to it a second and subsequent times. As soon as we become conscious of what is happening we are on the path to healing. Conscious awareness and witnessing with compassion is key to healing trauma, both within oneself and within others.

What Causes Trauma to Happen and Why Aren't Animals that are wild, Traumatised?

All mammals have the same response to danger, the same alarm system in the brain that causes them to take action to protect themselves, but humans end up traumatised whilst wild mammals seem not to unless they are caught and trapped. Domestic animals that are abused over a long period of time have the tendency to become traumatised also.

The reptilian, or hindbrain, is the part of the brain common to all mammals. In this part of the brain, we have two amygdalae which are extremely sensitive to any information coming into the brain via our five senses. This is an alarm system and the amygdalae will determine the nature of the information and whether or not it represents threatening circumstance that may endanger our lives. It is the same for all animals.

At the slightest stimulus, the amygdala will sound the alarm, 'DANGER! DANGER!'. They trigger the hypothalamus-pituitary-adrenal (HPA) axis in the brain that results in the body being flooded with neurotransmitters. This cascade of neurotransmitters in our bodies are designed to protect us. They do this by rapidly changing our physiology in terms of oxygen levels, heart rate, respiration, muscle tone, preparing us to take action to avoid deal with the danger.

Normal functions that happen when we are in a relaxed state, such as digestion and healthy immune function, are switched off. Other emergency states are switched on such as the 'active alert response', or 'fight and flight' and finally as a last, protective response, 'parasympathetic shutdown'. The neurotransmitters are communicating with the organs of your body, and functions such as heart rate, blood to the limbs, and breathing, change. You will be triggered into several possible responses. You may become very hot and agitated and want to fight or run away.

Either way, your limbs are powered up to do this very effectively. Or you may become deeply fearful and overwhelmed, cold, dissociated and maybe collapse. All states serve a survival purpose. The type of state you go into will depend upon a number of factors such as the nature of the threat, how traumatised you are already and how resourced you are and what emotional support you have and if you are able to feel safe and connected in that relationship.

What happens with wild animals, and how are humans similar?

This metaphor comes from the work of Dr. Peter Levine with slight changes.

Picture a scene on the plains of Africa! A herd of antelope are grazing peacefully. Suddenly, they all stop together, tighten their muscles and lift their heads to scent the air. Their eyesight and hearing sharpened. A hunting lion will cause the antelope to go on active alert once they sense the lion through sight or smell. Active alert is a heightened sense of awareness and tenseness in the body; an anxiety that something is about to happen. If the lion loses interest, the antelope will relax and continue to graze. However, if the lion starts to chase its prey, the antelope will be triggered into the fight-or-flight response. The blood is directed to the limbs and the heart beats faster. Breathing quickens and becomes fast and shallow. Tremendous power goes to the limbs so that the antelope can escape. It is this immense power and energy in the fight-or-flight mode that enables a mother to be able to lift a car off of her trapped child.

Not all animals run. Some animals and humans may turn to face their aggressor and begin to fight. The power in the limbs from the adrenaline makes them very angry. It is in this situation of intense rage that one person can kill another. Fight-or-flight is a powerful defence mechanism.

Coming back to the herd of antelope being chased by the lion, we find that if the lion gives up the chase and doesn't catch the antelope, then eventually the antelope will stop running and settle back to a normal relaxed state. If, however, the lion catches the antelope, then the third line of defence happens. The antelope goes into collapse. Sometimes, this will happen even before the antelope is caught. One moment it is running very fast and suddenly it can drop to the ground. It is as if it knows that all is lost. It switches gear into a last defensive response that may ultimately save its life. The antelope's body will become very cold as the blood withdraws from the limbs and the heart rate slows to an almost imperceptible level. The energy is withdrawn to the core of the antelope in a final attempt at surviving the attack. This is known as parasympathetic shock. The antelope appears as if dead, but is not dead. Should the lion eat the antelope at this stage, it will feel nothing as the antelope's body has become numb to the pain.

Humans in this state have been known to continue trying to help others whilst suffering terrible physical injury of which they are unaware because of the numbing effect. If the lion drags the antelope to a place and leaves it for its cubs to eat and the cubs don't turn up, the antelope will recover after a certain length of time. It will get up and start shaking; eventually, it will clear the overload of neurotransmitters from the cells and be finally back to normal again. This intense shaking represents the final phase of the defence cycle. It is a discharge of all the activation energy built up in the body of the antelope. It is now completely cleared from its body, and its muscles are relaxed, heart rate and respiration are back to normal, and its other autonomic functions, such as digestion and immune response, are operating normally.

The antelope has not been traumatised by its life-threatening experience!

This same nervous system response happens in all animals, including humans. However, humans are more complex and end up getting traumatised. The problem seems to be our frontal cortex that interferes with the protective functions of the reptilian brain. The frontal cortex is the part of the brain that is able to think and to reason. It is the part of the brain where socialisation takes place. It can over-ride the necessary final release of the activation cycle, causing us to be stuck in these intense energies of activation.

How many times have we been told 'not to cry' or 'pull yourself together' or 'it's not that bad' when bad things are happening? We rationalise ourselves and others, especially our children, out of the animal protective response and the autonomic nervous system becomes stuck in an unfinished cycle. Another factor is that this release cycle can be very intense, and we tend to block it when it starts to happen as it can feel uncomfortable and even frightening. We may also feel shame that we are getting out of control. We may even fear that we are becoming mentally unstable and that we will be rejected; rejection being the worst and most dangerous experience for a human being. Since humans are tribal animals, we need each other in order to be safe. If we are pushed out or rejected by others it is very traumatising.

And so, we as humans, largely don't shake the activation out of our bodies and we are left traumatised.

So, trauma is a frozen autonomic nervous system activation. We are stuck in defence mode.

We may be stuck endlessly in 'fight-or-flight' mode or 'active alert' or 'parasympathetic shock'. Often, we are stuck in all three at the same time.

If we take the metaphor of driving a car, it is as if we are trying to drive with both the accelerator and the brake jammed down simultaneously. The car is unable to drive, just the same as we can no longer direct our lives in the way that we could before we became traumatised. We may be endlessly oscillating between an anxiety state and depression, or flare up easily in anger and then collapse into helplessness. We may be triggered by the smallest thing without even realising it, and always be on the alert that something is going to go wrong at any moment. It is a very exhausting state to be in. Such an ongoing condition undermines the immune system and also leads to debilitating illness such as myalgic encephalomyelitis/ chronic fatigue syndrome (ME/CFS), or even perhaps attention deficit hyperactivity disorder (ADHD), as suggested by Dr Peter Levine, one of the first people to recognise the effects of trauma on humans, and to understand what was happening with the nervous system. Dr Gabor Mate talks in his book, 'When the Body Says No', about all chronic illness having roots in trauma.

This degree of trauma can happen as a result of a single life-threatening situation. However, often trauma can occur following much more complex situations that can begin very early in childhood or even in the womb. This kind of trauma is more complex to heal and it can feel like one's soul is lost, or a sense of self has never even existed. It can be a hugely devastating, existential experience that can hold a person in its grip. In this instance, it is so much more than the physical symptoms in the body of frozen trauma energy, such as would occur after a single traumatising event such as an accident or an attack. This kind of complex trauma with it's roots in our earliest period of development requires a multi-level treatment approach such as a combined psychotherapy with body work or body awareness focus and a great deal of compassion. This is the kind of therapeutic help you would find with Sensoria-motor Psychotherapy or Core Process Psychotherapy.

The following information will help you to be able to work with and heal your own trauma depending on the level of severity. If you are suffering from complex trauma you may need to seek further help and you can still combine with the information and methods below.

Frozen Trauma Energy and Somatic Experiencing:

Dr Peter Levine is a pioneer in trauma research. He discovered the very physical nature of trauma. He recognised the way that frozen energies are held in the body. from the uncompleted nervous system cycle and actions taken during the period of activation that were unable to be completed. An example is, if you put your arm out to protect yourself from falling and it wasn't successful and then you had a serious injury and was frozen in shock. He devised the method of 'Somatic Experiencing' as a way of completing and releasing the energies. His pioneering work has helped thousands of people. Somatic Experiencing is a way of creating a feedback system from the body to the autonomic nervous system, signaling to it that the dangerous event is now over and it can stop being on active alert. It also helps to complete actions that were not successful at the time of activation and to free the muscle tension and frozen energy in the limbs.

"I learnt how to create safety and strategies to feel as deeply into my body as it would allow, learning how to titrate and pendulate the pain."   *Julia Pennington*

Somatic Experiencing is a means of experiencing how the traumatising event is still held in the body, as signified by posture, gesture, thought processes, and emotion. You are no longer the 'you' that you were before the event. You have now embodied the experience of the traumatising event. It is frozen into your body.

At the moment that the traumatising event happened, time also froze and everything that was happening in that moment, what you were thinking, feeling, doing gets glued together. A new meaning gets glued into this stuck experience such as: "it is not safe to go out alone, I will get attacked". This new meaning now limits your life.

Dr. Peter Levine describes this as a condensed experience. When we are traumatised we become progressively more and more shut down because of these frozen energies and condensed experiential states of being.

Through Somatic Experiencing you can begin to track your sensations, thoughts, and emotions which are now compressed together, and learn what you are holding in your body. Before you can do this, however, you have to set up a physical sense of well-being as a resource. This is either by finding a feeling of comfort in the body, or by finding something outside of the body that creates a feeling of well-being, like looking at a calming picture or object.

Once this sensory foundation of resource has been created, unresolved actions of fight-or-flight, for instance, which are present in muscles, can be released by going through somatic exercises. It is important that this work is done slowly; unresolved experience or incomplete orientation to a dangerous situation needs to be identified somatically, and then, in a resourced way, released from the body. In this way, complex traumatic experiences can be healed. It is a body up approach with the focus on what the sensation is. It is not an approach of head down, working through emotions to get to the memories.

The focus is on re-regulating the nervous system by releasing the frozen trauma energies from the muscles as well as the condensed experience of locked emotion and new meaning that has been attached here. The trauma symptoms are arising from the animal part of the brain, so the key to unravelling and releasing them is also through that part of the brain; that which regulates sensation. The aim is to mobilise a sense of power and life energy where power was suddenly overwhelmed in a life-threatening situation. As frozen trauma energies are released, then sensation and greater freedom of movement will be experienced alongside a lessening of nervous system contraction into the intense feelings of panic, fear, anxiety, and anger. Gradually these feelings will lessen or be transformed, and a greater sense of relaxation and ease, more ability to be open to possible outcomes and feelings of happiness and even joy will return.

Somatic Experiencing is a wonderful modality for more simple trauma such as after an abuse or accident. If you are suffering more complex developmental trauma, Somatic Experiencing is still a very powerful modality in that it teaches nervous system regulation. This is a necessary first step in any kind of trauma healing.

"This exercise was profound for me, the combination of the trauma knowledge and then feeling into my body was a whole new experience. ....I found myself feeling for the first time in a very long time."
Julia Pennington

However in Developmental Trauma, then other kinds of psychotherapeutic integrative processes need to be compassionately facilitated by a skilled therapist that can witness and support their client. What this means is that there needs to be other emotional and psychological support within the context of therapy with a skilled psychotherapist that has skills also to work with the body. There needs to be a good relationship where safety is experienced in order to work with complexity of Developmental Trauma.

Triggers, and How They Take You Out of Your 'Window of Tolerance'

Once we have been traumatised, we can easily be activated into the autonomic nervous system responses described above. The brain has a way of noticing triggers and getting locked into believing that the same event is happening over and over again. For instance, if, just as you were about to have a car crash, you noticed the red scarf lying on the passenger seat, this image can become stuck, and remain unprocessed in the part of the brain responsible for memory, called the hippocampus.

Should you have survived the accident, the sight of a similar red scarf at a later date may trigger your brain into acting as if you are about to die. It could even just be the colour red that does this, or any scarf. The memory fragment has become stuck, 'undigested' in the hippocampus, as a result of the trauma. In a life-threatening situation, you may subliminally notice all kinds of things, that then become triggers for future activation.

It may be the sight of something, or it may be a smell, or a sound. You may not even know what the trigger is. Simply that you frequently get activated into a panic state, for no apparent reason.

As a young woman, I would go into shock and the freezing response whenever I was in an environment where a celebration was happening. It would be a trigger for the abandonment that I had experienced as a child where important events were not celebrated or honoured.

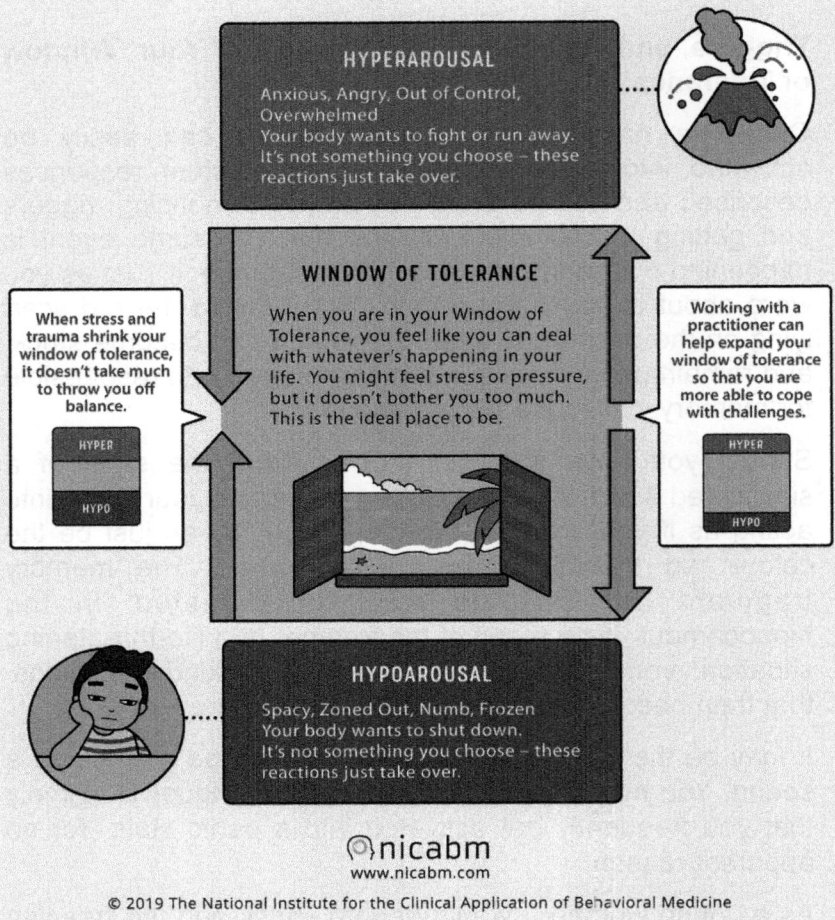

How Trauma Can Affect Your Window Of Tolerance

HYPERAROUSAL

Anxious, Angry, Out of Control, Overwhelmed
Your body wants to fight or run away.
It's not something you choose – these reactions just take over.

WINDOW OF TOLERANCE

When you are in your Window of Tolerance, you feel like you can deal with whatever's happening in your life. You might feel stress or pressure, but it doesn't bother you too much. This is the ideal place to be.

When stress and trauma shrink your window of tolerance, it doesn't take much to throw you off balance.

HYPER

HYPO

Working with a practitioner can help expand your window of tolerance so that you are more able to cope with challenges.

HYPER

HYPO

HYPOAROUSAL

Spacy, Zoned Out, Numb, Frozen
Your body wants to shut down.
It's not something you choose – these reactions just take over.

nicabm
www.nicabm.com

© 2019 The National Institute for the Clinical Application of Behavioral Medicine

Learning to recognise your triggers is helpful, as you can then begin to have the awareness that certain things cause you to feel in a particular way whilst at the same time knowing that what you are experiencing is a MEMORY of a dangerous event that happened in the past.

You are not about to die at the moment that you are triggered into that memory. By having some forewarning and awareness you create some psychological and somatic space so that you can decrease the activation of your nervous system before it ever skyrockets.

This is what is meant by 'managing your autonomic nervous system'. It is useful to be able to keep it within a 'window of tolerance' so that you can stay in your comfort zone, and not fly off into being either in 'fight-or-flight' or 'parasympathetic shock.'

The ability to do this will depend upon the individual, and the degree and complexity of the trauma. For some people, they may not be able to spot their triggers or else even whilst spotting them they cannot get control of the activation. Some triggers can also be internal such as increased heart beat or specific tightening of a muscle. However, it is useful to understand the process and attempt to have that awareness and control, but not to be self-criticising if not immediately successful. Above all, kindness to self and compassion are the most important aspects of the healing process.

Learning to recognise your window of tolerance will help you to heal. Even if you can't spot the individual triggers, you will become more aware of when you are not comfortable anymore.

What is Recapitulation, Counter Recapitulation and Traumatic Recycling?

I have described how traumatic patterns keep repeating themselves, why does this happen? Once we have trauma in our bodies, the brain is living in 'trauma time'. It is continually in the past, re-enacting the emergency response necessary to survive the impending death. When your body is being flooded with chemicals causing you to fight or flee or collapse for no apparent reason, it is very confusing and very distressing. We are continually, without conscious choice, acting on false information. Information from the past, from a life threatening event that is no longer happening. However, a small trigger, that reminds you of that event, gives the brain the feeling that it is still happening. This is a false perception. Once traumatised, our perceptions are distorted and it is hard to know what is reality. We are continually reliving the past and making our choices from those experiences in the past.

Many people have flashbacks, and it is entirely possible to heal them. The more you understand what is happening the more successful you will be. Already, the knowledge that you have acquired up to this point will begin to help you.

Flashbacks:

So what are flashbacks?

A trigger, can take you back to the original traumatising situation and you may also have flashback images in your waking reality to the event that caused the problem. Or you may have nightmares. Flashbacks can be memory fragments, emotional experiences, or whole scenes playing out in front of you. Like hallucinations, they are entirely convincing that they are happening in the present moment. A typical flashback is when a war veteran, hearing a sudden loud noise, instantly reacts as if under fire again, and turns to take offensive action or hide from the attack. It could be a car backfiring or other loud noise that triggers him into this.

Flashbacks can be obvious like this, or intense emotions can flare up in a relationship or interaction with someone that are out of context with the situation. You may be totally convinced that the situation in question has caused the intense feelings.

Thomas Hubl recommends spending time at the end of each day, reflecting on any situations that you had during the day with 'difficult people'. What was it about them that was 'difficult' and when has this happened to you before? How many times? What can you do within yourself to change it?

You may start blaming the other person of doing something hurtful or harmful to you and make them responsible for a situation that is not even happening. The reality is that you are having emotional flashbacks from a previous traumatic event. A time perhaps when you were harmed by someone or didn't feel safe when you were little because you did not have a secure attachment with a parent. This can cause enormous conflict within a relationship and then an escalation into another bad situation possibly such as the eventual break up of a relationship.

Flashbacks are all a result of unprocessed memory, held in the hippocampus which is the part of the brain responsible for filing away memory. It is a bit like the memory of what happened before has not been properly digested and keeps coming up. Once traumatised, the hippocampus is not able to do its job very well as it gets affected by cortisol levels. Normally it will process memory and file it away in appropriate compartments so that the brain knows that an event is fully over.

Unprocessed memory continually cause you to act as if it is still happening. This is what is called 'trauma time'.

These flashbacks may cause you to become extremely phobic and generally fearful of life itself. Nothing and nowhere is safe. It is hard to understand that actually the event that caused the problem is now over and done with. The brain is continually re-running the past event as if it were the present because it is stuck, unprocessed in the brain. It may entirely convince you that your life in the present moment is totally unsafe. The fact that you are continually in a perceived state of imminent danger, limits your choices about how you may live.

It may cause you to make bad choices that actually bring further traumatic experiences to you. For instance, if you constantly feel unsafe where you are and then run away to somewhere else without proper judgement, then you can bring yourself into more complex situations equally unsafe. In this way the trauma spirals and you keep repeating the same thing over.

In this way, a continual cycle of trauma can happen. You may be living your life from this 'place' and be bringing up your family as if they are in danger. Trauma in your own body/mind system can lead to all sorts of antisocial behaviour, child abuse, and violence. It can also lead to addictions as a means of relieving the stress of the trauma.

Children brought up by traumatised parents are unable to embody a sense of safety and well-being. They can be continually overwhelmed or stressed by the traumatic reactions of their parents. In cases where the parents have become addicted, or have other obsessive behaviours in order to compensate and modulate the unresolved trauma energies in their system, the children are having to cope with a completely chaotic environment.

It can feel as if you are going 'crazy' because of the incoherence in the relationships. These same children may have cortisol levels that are inadequate in supporting them through high levels or stress as a result of genetic changes passed on to them by their traumatised parents. These same parents may also have modelled obsessive, violent, or depressed and helpless behaviour.

It is no wonder that they themselves become traumatised, and then, in time, pass this on to their own children. For this reason, it is important to take steps to heal yourself. The lives of future generations are dependent on what you do here and now to heal yourself.

In addition, the 'field' or energy of trauma itself can somehow draw more traumatic events of a similar nature to you for you to experience. It is hard to say at this present moment how this happens. In some respects, as I said earlier, it is thought that the psyche or soul does this. I think that there are two factors at work here. For instance, psychological and emotional patterns develop around traumatic experiences, particularly those that happen in the prenatal stages.

One of the things that happened to me was that I was stuck in a life and death situation in the birth canal. It felt that I would not be able to survive, no matter what I did. I had to do something really quickly and work really hard or else I was going to die. It left an imprint in my nervous system of extreme anxiety. I would have a surge of adrenaline triggered whenever I was in a situation that triggered the 'stuck' feeling in my life. I would then work very hard, even to the cost of my physical well being to get out of the feeling.

Consequently, I have been in many situations where I have felt stuck and helpless in my life, and I have had to work really hard to get through them. In my attempt to counter these stuck feelings by working hard, I found that I was overextending myself and having poor boundaries. So there was another lesson to learn here in my healing process to help me grow towards being a balanced, boundaried person. This process took a lot of self reflection and awareness.

It seems that the psyche is continually drawing forth situations to re-pattern the original traumatic one. In my case, the mechanism being, that at an unconscious level I am choosing to do things that then put me under that kind of pressure where I then feel I have to fight for my survival.

In doing so, I achieve great results and am successful at what I do but there is a cost to my physical body in that I have physically and emotionally over-extended and then collapse or make bad decisions that bring more difficulty. In learning balance and boundaries, I meet the difficult stuck situations by resourcing myself and reflecting on what is bringing this situation up. What is it really about? If it requires an action, how can I do that in a way that is not causing me harm in any way?

How can I achieve goals in a measured way and continue to be successful without sacrificing myself or ending in a physical or emotional collapse? This process has taken me years and has required deep introspection as well as a lot of support along the way.

Counter recapitulation.

It is also possible to have a pattern of counter recapitulation from an early traumatic event. This is a pattern where you avoid, at all cost, ever doing anything that is going to recreate the feeling of the first situation. However, although you avoid the intense reaction, the avoidance approach is equally charged, and not likely to be a 'healed' approach to your life. It may mean that you go through life trying to avoid anything that can give you a suggestion of difficulty. Always trying to stay safe can totally limit creativity and exploration and end up being very bland and fearful. It may leave you feeling isolated or unfulfilled.

Trauma energy field.

As well as the psyche bringing around the trauma again to heal it, there also seems to be a 'field' of energy causing a repetition of the traumatic event. It can happen that the same kind of event can play over in disconnected situations.

For instance, the burning of the hotel in the Nazi massacre and the seemingly unrelated fires in my house. There was also a fire in the house prior to my buying it, making a total of three fires here. Perhaps there was an energy field of horror and fire created with the first massacre that left its imprint on the valley?

I also wonder if this had deeper roots since the valley is on the edge of the Cathar region. This is another story that I won't go into here! In a nutshell, the Cathars were massacred over a period of 200 years by the Pope in Medieval times for daring to step aside outside of the doctrine of the Catholic Church and experience divinity in their own way. Thousands of them were burnt at the stake. So we have the horrific theme here again in the same area of France.

Another example is the car crash that I was in that kept repeating, making a total of three crashes. How could it be that I had 3 separate crashes that were not caused by me? Somewhere in the energy field something was happening that I was not conscious of. It stopped when I really began to be conscious of a lot of things in my life that weren't working for me. In this same example, children of parents that have had a particular kind of accident can have similar accidents.

How do we heal this this traumatic energy field? It is often happening at what Thomas Hubl calls the Collective Trauma level. He teaches about the need of consciousness at this level. Groups of people can begin the healing process by examining and exploring the events together. What are their individual experiences of it and how do these experiences overlap into the Collective? This is a process that can expand into Global Social Witnessing.

Witnessing and bringing conscious awareness to what is happening, is a very powerful way of healing trauma, especially when done with true compassion. It works at an individual level when you sit and reflect on what was it in yourself that helped to create the 'difficult situation' . It can also work when you are a group exploring together the events that you witness.

One of the most important aspects of this is to take personal responsibility. We are all powerful creators and we create our reality moment by moment. When we blame others for something that has happened, we are evading our personal responsibility. When you stop finding that there is a problem outside of yourself and begin to explore within yourself, then you have the power to change the things that are causing pain. Healing Trauma is about finding that power to take action again, rather than feeling disempowered, helpless and blaming external situations.

Are you aware of such things in your life?
If so, take heart, becoming conscious of this
is an important step to healing it. You too can
heal just the same way that many other
people have healed.

CHAPTER 2

The Symptoms of Trauma

Please be aware that as I talk about the symptoms of trauma that you may become activated yourself. If this is the case, then skip this section until you feel sufficiently resourced to read it. If it is a mild activation, then remind yourself that you are safe and that the past is over and done with. Stop reading a while, walk around the room and find something that is pleasant to look at or enjoyable to pick up. Immerse yourself in the comfortable feelings that you get whilst doing this. When you are ready, you can go back to reading what I have written here, all the time taking care to notice if it is triggering you.

Early or Hidden Trauma:

Some symptoms of trauma may be very apparent and you know that you are suffering from it, whilst others are not. You may have had similar symptoms for a long time and be so used to them that you identify them as being 'just the way you are'. It depends when the traumatic event has happened and whether symptoms that are present have started a short time after the life-threatening event. Some events, such as pre-natal trauma, may take some conscious research to begin to understand and heal them. The mainstream belief is that we have no awareness or memory, or that we are not even human until after we are born, so how could we have trauma from that time?

Up until only a few years ago, it was believed that babies could not feel pain. How wrong all that is. Indeed, the earliest traumas from preconception are often the most profound and may lead to a whole lifetime of not feeling safe or welcome, or sure of the meaning of your existence.

Trauma that has happened in childhood, or as a result of an attack in later years, can also be deeply buried in the psyche. If the trauma has been so great that it has led to parasympathetic shock and dissociation, then you may have no awareness whatsoever that anything life-threatening has happened to you. There are many examples of people that have been sexually abused as a child and they have no conscious memory until something triggers the memory, years later as adults. One such example is when women give birth to their own children, or if they have surgery of some kind. This can be a highly triggering event which brings memories of early sexual abuse to the surface. Similarly, dentistry work can also trigger memories of sexual abuse.

If you have reactions to situations which are out of proportion with the events that are happening, then you might suspect that something else is being suppressed by your unconscious. That 'something' will be putting a 'charge' into, and influencing, your life and freedom. It is not possible to make happy, free choices when fear and anxiety are holding you back. In healing these traumas, it is not necessary to dig up the memory, but it is necessary to have an awareness that something is not right and that your nervous system is operating as if you are under threat. Indications that such a thing is going on is if you have a belief that you had a 'normal' childhood and yet you have a history of nightmares, anxiety, or depression. Or if you are easily upset in certain situations without understanding why. Or if you have phobia's or addictions. These symptoms are not there just because you got unlucky, they are there because your body and psyche are trying to heal something that happened a long time ago, and it has got stuck.

If you have experiences like these, they need you to help it along and the symptoms will clear. You yourself may need help with this because often these experiences are so deeply rooted that it takes skill and compassion to be able to heal them. If this is the case, I advise you to get the assistance of some Trauma Resolution Therapy. I personally offer this at Healing Waters Sanctuary (www.healing-waters.co.uk), or you can look for someone who is either a body-focused psychotherapist, such as Pat Ogden who does Sensorimotor Psychotherapy, or a Somatic Experiencing Therapist as taught by Dr Peter Levine.

Surgery or Medical Interventions:

Sometimes you may have experienced something that is really traumatic, and yet you are told that it is normal and therefore your symptoms are not recognised as a trauma. Examples of this are medical interventions and surgery. All surgery is, by its nature, traumatic. Just because you have been given an anaesthetic and you didn't feel it, doesn't mean that it wasn't experienced by your body as being life-threatening.

It WAS life-threatening, and it is going to give you trauma symptoms. They may be mild and with sufficient time they might pass, but also the chances are that they are severe. The danger is when the medical profession decide that you are 'just suffering from a bout of depression' and give you medication for it. The medication doesn't have much chance of helping and may bring more harmful effects. The surgery may have felt really overwhelming to your body and on that physical level would have been life threatening without the care that went alongside it.

These feelings of overwhelm can leave you feeling flat and depressed and may eventually without help turn into an ongoing depression. This is because the overwhelm caused your body to go into parasympathetic shock that then became a chronic state. Feelings of overwhelm that you are about to die inevitably appear as depression. Sometimes after surgery, the symptoms of trauma are very great and, together with the painkilling drugs such as morphine, you may suffer attacks of paranoia, dissociation, terror, disorientation, anxiety, and fear. I have had a personal conversation with a surgeon who related the story of how the medical profession is not equipped to teach their staff how to look out for and prepare patients for the ensuing trauma from the effects of surgery and drugs.

If you are about to have surgery, do have this discussion with your consultant, and if they don't acknowledge it, then make sure that you have some emotional and trauma resolution support.

Traumatic reactions deepen as more and more life-threatening events are loaded onto your nervous system so it is vital that you clear this before it gets worse. It was only after my third car accident that I realised that I was suffering from PTSD.

Veterans of War or Emergency Services:

Another area of sadness where, in the past, people have not been acknowledged for the trauma that they are suffering, is with veterans of war. For a very long time, many millions of young men and women have been persuaded, forced, or manipulated into going to fight in wars that are happening or have happened, on our planet.

This has had disastrous, largely unacknowledged, consequences on the lives of these young people and on their families, should they have been lucky enough to live to

> Fortunately, because of the research of Dr Bessel van der Kolk and the ground-breaking skill and work of Dr Peter Levine with Somatic Experiencing, there is now a lot of help for war veterans. It is entirely possible to heal using these methods..

return home. In addition to this, war has caused immense trauma in the lives of the innocent populations that have been caught in the war. Further, the harmful effects of the war have been passed down through several generations. At this point, everyone on our planet has been traumatised by wars that we have had some connection with, either directly or through witnessing war via film or story, or by being a descendent of someone who was.

PTSD has only in recent times been recognised as a symptom of war. Only a generation ago, when a soldier suffered the traumatic effects of war, he or she was named as being a coward and forced to continue fighting.

(To me, war is an obscenity and quite unnecessary. It is a politically manipulated event for the creation of profit whilst our young people are duped into believing that it will bring a change for the better. If not for the world, then maybe in their own lives because of the 'career' opportunities that it creates.........excuse my rant!)

My brother was one such young man who was told that he would be given an education if he signed up to go and fight in Northern Ireland. He ended up very traumatised and eventually committed suicide. Millions of veterans return from these wars, their lives destroyed, the lives of their families broke. Such suffering has generally been unacknowledged. There is now a little recognition, but nowhere near enough help for them to heal these difficult traumas. Young people are even traumatised by the 'draft' that signs them up to go and fight. I know a number of men that had their lives turned upside down by the Vietnam War. It was challenging to escape the war machine, often causing them to be imprisoned if they refused to fight. What a system of evil and how it prays on the vulnerabilities of our young people!

Soldiers and Sailors have also been very traumatised in nuclear testing, and also dealing with accidents such as Fukushima, which has caused massive radiation damage to their physical bodies as well as the trauma to their nervous systems. Firefighters, police officers, and emergency services people are also often traumatised but may not know that they are. If you have had any of these occupations and experience symptoms such as chronic fatigue, anxiety, depression, nightmares, irritability, mood swings, addictions, anger attacks, or rage, it may be a result of trauma. Likewise, if you are the partner or child of someone within these occupations you also may be traumatised. Vicarious traumatisation is a common experience. Living with a veteran who is having flashbacks of the war, and who suffers violent rages, is a life-threatening experience for the rest of the family. The intensity of the unresolved trauma in the soldier's nervous system may cause him/her to physically attack their family when triggered into a blind rage.

Addiction:

What are the links between trauma and addiction? Dr Gabor Mate, one of the world's experts on addiction, with many years of first-hand experience of working with addicts, says that not all traumatised people are addicted but all addicted people are traumatised.

When we think of addiction, we tend to think of an addict as a person with a hardcore reliance on, and usage of, drugs such as heroin, cocaine, opiates, crystal meth, and alcohol, to name a few. However, Dr Mate talks about the usage of any kind of activity, even apparently harmless things - like his own addiction to shopping for music CDs - can become self-destructive if the pursuit of that activity or substance is done at the cost of everything else. Addiction always has a negative consequence and it is often the addicted person's family and friends that feel the suffering first. For the addicted person, there may not appear to be a problem at first, since the aim of the substance/activity usage is to dampen their own pain and suffering. It could be that this has been going on for a long time, and they are not even aware that there is anything wrong with the behaviour until the negative effects are finally felt, and the toll on their lives and relationships begin to be apparent. By that time, the dependency can be so great, and the need to control the pain so intense, that the addicted person will sacrifice everything, and perhaps even steal or kill, in order to maintain the addiction.

Addiction is a need to create a state of being using the substance or activity that will cancel out the pain of the suffering. This happens as a result of the dopamine (the neurotransmitter responsible for pleasure and motivation) being released in the brain when the addictive activity or substance is used. Anyone with intense energies of trauma in their body, and the consequent physical, emotional, and psychological pain, may well turn to the use of substances or behaviours that distract from, and dampen the pain. Both physical and emotional pain are experienced in the same part of the brain, and emotional and psychological pain can be just as intense as physical pain.

Addictions can be found in all sorts of forms. Some of them are judged and even criminalised, whilst others are even praised and seen as a virtue. In this respect, I am thinking of the workaholic; a state of being that we often encourage people to achieve, particularly in the medical profession. Other commonly accepted addictions are the use of foods, coffee, tea, and the pursuit of sporting activities. Commonly also practised and not often recognised is shopping addiction (or consumerism, which is the cornerstone of our culture). Sexual addiction, pornography, and smoking are some others which are sometimes frowned upon but still allowable.

How to heal addiction:

There are many treatment centres for ~~the~~ hardcore addictions, as well as ten-step programmes such as Narcotics and Alcoholics Anonymous. These programmes can be life-saving and have helped many people, but the tendency is that people who have problems with addiction can easily slip back into the behaviour unless the other deep emotional work is done. It is important to understand that doing something to stop an addictive behaviour is not the same as healing the addiction. If we attempt to end the addiction ~~by~~ withdrawing the substance or activity, the behaviour will return in another form. Addiction is like the snakes on the head of the Hydra; each snake that is lopped off will just spring back again. The way to heal addiction is to get to the roots of the suffering. For this process, it is necessary to have a great deal of compassion, particularly as addiction is so stigmatised.

The path to healing addiction is through consciousness. This applies to all of us. Many, many people have addictive patterns or personalities of which they are unaware, but their partners, children, or loved ones will be feeling the effects. Beginning to become conscious of how addiction is playing out in your life is the first step to healing it. If you are deeply in the grip of any kind of addiction, you will first need to stop the addictive behaviour, particularly if it involves

By reading the previous information you will have learnt that addiction is not a bad thing to be ashamed of. Neither is it a disease that you cannot recover from. Addiction is something that can happen to anyone in immense pain. Addiction is an attempt to dull the pain.

Now that you know this, you can use the tools and exercises in this book to heal that pain.

"The resourcing exercise was greatly liberating as it enabled me to see my addiction (to alcohol) as a resource rather than as a demon to be battled with. These days, if I have an intense craving for alcohol, I know that something deeply painful has been

using mind-altering substances and/or ones that dampen down the natural opiates in your body, such as heroin. It is not possible to become conscious as long such substances are taking over your nervous system. Befriending your addictive behaviour helps to change it. Understanding its function in your life gives you a better chance of healing rather than feeling bad about doing it.

It is important to get a lot of support and to do some deep emotional and trauma therapy as part of healing the pain that gives rise to your addictive behaviour. When you are deeply in the addictive pattern you may not be aware of what lies underneath the addiction. You may not be aware of the pain. It is only when you stop the addiction that the pain comes up and the awareness of what is causing it will become apparent after much therapy. The addiction masks the pain as it creates dopamine, a neurotransmitter that gives a 'feel good' affect in your body. It is important to get some good help if you are suffering with addiction. In that respect, many activities and exercises in this book will be helpful. You may also want to seek out other therapy work as described at the end of this book.

Families with Addictions and Abuse:

Being the wife, husband or child of someone who has an alcohol or substance addiction-is a very traumatising experience. Human beings need to have solid loving relationships with dependable caring people. The closest people in their lives need to be people that create safety and well-being for them.

If your closest family is often or always under the influence of a drug or alcohol, or even an addictive activity such as gambling, spending or working too hard, they are not able to provide a safe environment for you. They will be emotionally unavailable and very unpredictable. Their behaviour will be inconsistent as there may be many hours when under the influence of the addiction when they are not relating to your needs. They may lack empathy and not be able to attune accurately to you.

This is a core need for young children and can be very damaging when it is not available. You may often feel at risk with them since their boundaries may be poor. They may cause things to happen in your family situation that you need protection from. It may be that you are too frightened to express the minimum of normal behaviour around them for fear of an angry reaction or a withdrawal of their attention. In addition, they may be violent and abusive. Children are dependent upon their parents to regulate their nervous system. An addicted person often has difficulties with their own nervous system regulation so will not be able to co-regulate with their children.

The same may apply with a intimate partner. People suffering from addiction, are themselves, the victims of trauma, but knowing this provides little comfort in the face of threatening behaviours and lack of empathy or attunement.

If you are living in a family with a member with addictive patterns it will be a situation where you are traumatised. You may suffer an enormous amount of fear and anxiety or other emotional and physical suffering. How is it possible to cope with such a situation? Often you may end up developing various coping strategies. It may lead you to eating disorders or even substance abuse yourself. It is vital to get help and to remove yourself from the situation if at all possible. Often family members try to change the behavior of the addicted person but it is enormously difficult. Finally they usually have to realise that they are powerless in the situation. It may happen that you are being 'gas lit' when you try to change this behaviour and you begin to feel more and more helpless. It is important to seek therapy help yourself, especially if you can find help from organisations specialising in addiction. You may also just have to leave the relationship for your own safety. You did not cause the situation; you cannot change it. You did not choose it. You can only choose to put yourself in a safe environment where you can heal yourself.

Another very traumatising family situation is where one or both of the parents are very self-absorbed or narcissistic and the child is either physically or emotionally neglected.

Narcissistic parents cannot accurately attune to their children's needs. They will often lack empathy or give occasional empathy. Oftentimes they may treat their children as objects. They only value the child as an accessory to themselves, to enhance their own appearance to others. They may gas-light the child when she/he attempts to share their pain about the lack of real relationship.

Like growing up in a family with addiction, this kind of family environment leads to an inner emptiness and great anxiety. Abandonment may be experienced as a core issue and great loneliness. Being brought up with this kind of emotional neglect is probably more traumatising than physical abuse, especially if the child is made to feel that there is no reason for their feelings of suffering and that there is something wrong with them for feeling this way. It can be really difficult to build safe relationships with others if there was no safe relationship with your own parents.

"I learnt how to move in and out of my emotional pain, when I learnt about developmental trauma, for me that was powerful, now I truly understand what activation is. I realised I was activated in every moment; I was constantly on high alert."
Julia Pennington

Developmental Trauma:

Traumatised children are often the result of what is known as 'developmental trauma'. A human baby is more vulnerable than any other mammal. We are very undeveloped when we are born, and for the first nine months after birth, we are still highly vulnerable and require a lot of care both physically and emotionally. We are highly dependent upon our 'primary carers'. This is usually our mother but may be a father or adopted guardian.We rely upon them so that our fundamental core needs can be met.

This is vital for the development of important centres in the brain that are connected with relationship and learning.

The primary need is that of 'attachment'. Should this not be secure, it can cause a major traumatic wounding. Attachment damage can have a big impact on later life and lead to difficulty in forming safe happy relationships.

According to the research of Dr Laurence Heller, other core needs are those of 'attunement', 'autonomy', 'trust', and 'love and sexuality'. Each time one of these core needs are neglected it leads to a particular kind of psychic wound and traumatic damage. Healing these kinds of traumas are complex and require a highly skilled therapist. However, somatic experiencing is helpful as a first step because it teaches people who are suffering how to manage their nervous system, and to maintain it within a 'window of comfort and tolerance'.

"As Dr Gabor Mate says, 'It's never too late to discover you had an unhappy childhood', and of course I'd normalised what was, in reality, a hellish childhood lived mainly in the adrenaline response as I was frequently left at the mercy of two older bullying brothers in the absence of parents who were always busy working. Just the conscious awareness of this was in itself a great release."
Rachel Elnaugh

Dr Gabor Mate also writes extensively about Developmental Trauma, Attachment Damage, and Attunement Damage. In his research he has found that the lack of good, focussed, caring parenting, leads to problems with the way parts of the child's brain develops.

This can cause issues of Attention Deficit Disorder as well as problems in relationships and behavioural self-regulation. He writes and lectures extensively on the problems caused by 'stressed parenting'. He says that a parent or guardian can totally love a child but if they themselves are highly stressed, the child will still not get the kind of reflection and care that it needs for normal, healthy development.

If you are feeling alone, unworthy or not good enough, and you can't make sense of it because you feel that you had a good upbringing and loving parents, it may be that you just didn't get the kind of parenting that a child needs to be happy and healthy. It is time to stop blaming yourself. This is an important step in order to heal this condition.

Accidents:

Accidents are not always, but often can be, very traumatising, depending on the severity of them and your state of health at the time. I was in considerable shock after the first car accident that I had, but I didn't understand about trauma. I was not physically injured but was really shaken up and disoriented. Each accident was a progressively worse ordeal for my nervous system. After the third one, I could not sleep at night and my vision was really disturbed as if I was looking through broken glass. I was extremely sensitive to sound, and the unexpected approach of people alarmed me; I would jump out of my skin.

The worst thing was that people would laugh or make fun of me when I was alarmed in this way as if I were crazy. This is secondary traumatisation - when people ridicule you for being traumatically disturbed. It happens to a lot of people without anyone understanding how serious it is. Secondary traumatisation also happens when other people tell you to 'snap out of it' or 'pull yourself together' or say 'it's not that bad'. This lack of compassion and understanding is very wounding when you are already so vulnerable.

The other symptoms that I had were terrible noises of roaring and hissing in my ears. I would also physically shake a lot. The doctors at the hospital found no physical injury and could not understand why I was distressed. They treated me as if I was malingering. Extreme sensitivity to sensory information like light or sound or physical sensations is a common symptom of trauma. I was so sound sensitive that it was unbearable for me to put the indicators on in the car; the sound of them clicking whilst indicating was awful.

The other effect was that I was terrified to drive after the last accident. This was particularly bad when I had to overtake another vehicle. I would feel like I was going to pass out with terror. I had to work on this for a long time when I was driving. I would take deep breaths in, and long out-breaths. Long out breaths bring down the levels of adrenaline in the body so that I could be a lot more relaxed and focused.

This is an important part of self regulation. I also used important Somatic Experiencing tools with which I eventually cured myself . Somatic refers to the body and being in touch with the body through using the five senses. This is called sensory awareness. When distressed, in order to self regulate, (I.e be calm again) focussing on senses of comfort, wellbeing and safety are vitally important in calming the nervous system and self regulating to calmness. I would do this when I was driving. I would take long out breaths, notice the comfort of my bottom on the seat. Feel my hands on the steering wheel and begin telling myself that I was safe prior to the moment of overtaking. I would start to really focus on my breathing and my somatic awareness as I moved into the overtaking lane.

By continually grounding myself, feeling my body heavy on the seat of the car, and noticing the feeling of the steering wheel in my hand. I learnt to move my eyes around as I was passing the other vehicle. I would need to focus on the roadway ahead and then change to look to the side and then ahead again. I knew that above all not to look down to the side of the vehicle that I was passing. If I did, it would cause my eyes to lock and I would become highly activated and in danger of totally dissociating. The eyes are very important when self regulating and bringing yourself out of a state of activation. This is called orientating and it is what all animals do to check out the environment for safety or danger. When highly activated the eyes get stuck in a narrow band width. If you can move your eyes all around you can return a sense of safety to the body. Eventually, after about a year of doing this, the terror stopped and my nervous system returned to normal. From then on I could drive safely and without fear.

Witnessing the Death or Suffering of Others:

Seeing someone else being injured or dying can be terribly distressing and very traumatic. By this, I don't mean the natural and timely death that happens in loving surroundings; although it is very upsetting to lose someone that you love in any circumstances, it is the sudden tragic death in shocking circumstances which can be traumatising. I know several people that have witnessed the suicide of others and they were left traumatised for years. By this I don't mean that they saw it happen, (this would be even worse) but that someone close to them committed suicide. After this happened, their lives were turned upside down. They became very phobic about going to certain places which reminded them of the event. They were also very distressed about the fact that they had failed to help the person. It is a common feeling, after something like this or a terrible accident where others were killed, that the survivor or witness is tormented with the feeling that if only they had 'done something' or 'not done such and such' things would have been different and people would not have died. The truth is that you are never able to help in the awful moment of that sudden and unthinkable thing happening. Finding yourself in such a situation, where someone is going to take their own life, is so traumatic that you immediately go into a freezing terror-filled shutdown and can't function efficiently enough to prevent what is happening. Firemen and other emergency services personnel are very liable to be traumatised as a result of the work that they do in rescuing people who are trying to commit suicide or who are in a terrible accident or other emergency situation. Traumatisation of people in these services is commonplace, especially after they have had to deal with many people who have suffered horrendous deaths.

The symptoms of trauma are many and varied; but the important point to take from this chapter is that you are not bad, you are not broken, and you can heal.

All humans get traumatised, and it is the lack of understanding about trauma that has caused people like you to suffer. Now that you have this knowledge, you are on the path to healing yourself.

CHAPTER 3

Healing from Trauma

Trauma seriously limits your life and your choices. The experience of being traumatised can make you very miserable and you may not know why you are suffering.

If you are traumatised, you may be living in a world of terror and anxiety, which can lead to the creation of all sorts of unhealthy coping mechanisms such as alcohol abuse or OCD. You may not even know that you are traumatised. In addition, you could be giving yourself a really hard time over the feelings that you are having, and be very self-critical and judgmental. Those people who have had the worst traumas seem to be the hardest on themselves. I have known women who were terribly abused as children and be very critical of themselves because they can't get their life together and function well, or because they made some bad choices and which made things worse for themselves.

On the other hand, I had a client who had been really badly abused as a child and she totally turned her life around and did some amazing things to help other women.

People abused in childhood are very poorly equipped to make life-affirming choices about anything. Not only has the nervous system been traumatised, but the

social nervous system that relates to loving bonded relationships has also been damaged. In addition, there has been no clear modelling for normal relationships with good boundaries.

Trauma is largely unrecognised by mainstream medical practice, and when people show up with the symptoms of trauma they are frequently given anti-depressants or other drugs, and likely labelled as 'mentally ill'. This is particularly true in childhood trauma where children are given a plethora of diagnostic labels for behaviour such 'Oppositional Defiant Disorder' or ADHD, but it is never acknowledged by the medical establishment in the USA that they could be suffering from PTSD. Dr Bessel van der Kolk, a clinician, psychotherapist and trauma researcher with years of experience, campaigned and submitted extensive research about childhood trauma and strongly proposed that this diagnosis should be included in the Diagnostic and Statistical Manual, Fourth Edition (DSM-IV) but without success. Thus childhood developmental trauma is still only randomly acknowledged.

In the UK, if you are suffering trauma symptoms, you might be recommended to a psychotherapist and offered Cognitive Behavioural Therapy (CBT). CBT focusses upon changing peoples' underlying beliefs about themselves, and in so doing, is thought to change behaviour. Dr Bessel van der Kolk says that this is largely unhelpful in healing trauma. There is not a direct pathway from the thinking part of the brain to the reptilian brain which is where the trauma activation is originating from. Therefore, trying to think different thoughts, although useful in some ways - particularly later in the process of healing trauma - is not useful as the primary step of trauma healing.

In the 1960s there seemed to be a breakthrough in understanding and working with the intense feelings of trauma. Up until that time any kind of emotional problem was largely ignored and people were taught to suppress their feelings, or be 'psycho-analysed out of them'. Intense feeling is still largely discouraged by society, thus more deeply embedding trauma into our nervous systems, causing us to be driven by the symptoms of it. In doing this we become doubly ashamed that we cannot function as 'adult' human beings. We are driven by secret cravings, phobias, and addictions. Repetitive mental patterns, extreme anger, collapse, and depression. We try to hide these feelings of not coping as it is shameful. We suppress them so that the outside world can believe that we are sociable lovable people. We cling to our masks, losing our connection with our authentic selves since we are terrified of anyone knowing what is really going on with us. The shame of our situations is often unbearable.

In the 1960s, Primal Therapy was created by Arthur Janov. It seemed that he had made a breakthrough in enabling people to heal from their 'neuroses' as a result of repressed childhood traumas. The therapy encouraged individuals to access their emotions which then lead to a traumatic activation. The belief was that the more that you screamed and cried the better you would be. It was analogous to lancing a boil.

The emotions were believed to be the suppuration that had built up and the screaming would release everything and you could then heal. What was not understood, was that this activation would lead to further re-traumatisation. Once you are traumatised, it takes less and less to traumatise you again because your nervous system is already overloaded. As you get activated into intense emotions, the brain cannot differentiate between the original event and the replay of it through accessing the intense emotions of the event. The primitive brain reacts to the intense emotions experienced and interrupts them as further proof of danger. It will respond by flooding your system with more neurotransmitters to put you into fight-or-flight and parasympathetic shock, causing you to become even more traumatised. Consequentially, the intense primal therapy of Janov proved to be re-traumatising, unfortunately, there are still many people to this day that advocate this approach to healing.

As I write this book there is a growing trend of people turning to substances such as Ayahuasca which they also call 'plant medicine' as a means to healing trauma. It is felt to do this because it opens up the individual to intense experiences and insights about themselves and larger spiritual dimensions. Like the work done with Janov, it has grave drawbacks in its therapeutic use because of the likelihood of causing deeper traumatisation. Unfortunately because Dr. Gabor Mate, Addiction and Trauma specialist, has himself endorsed it's use, it is felt that it is a beneficial treatment. Dr. Peter Levine describes it as a tool like any other if used in the right way, however Dr. Bessel van der Kolk is interested in the use of certain psycho active drugs such as MDMA if explored under strict protocols to determine efficacy. Dr. Mate makes it quite clear that the use of Ayahuasca is something that would only be taken once or at the most twice in a year and under strict supervision. There would be a long period of the trauma therapy prior to taking it and another long period after it's use to fully integrate the experience. Anything else is dangerous as it opens the psyche to intense experience that cannot be adequately processed and may lead to psychosis.

Additionally it may also become an addiction through its repeated use. This is the same as any other drug, which it is, even if it gets named 'plant medicine'. At the current time there are individuals running groups to take this drug. Often large numbers of people attend over a weekend and pay a lot of money for an experience that is potentially dangerous since there is very little supervision and no therapy of the nature that the Trauma experts such as Dr

Gabor Mate, Dr Bessel van Der Kolk and Dr. Peter Levine would endorse. The participants are encouraged to repeat the experience on a regular basis. Each episode of such intense experience can add a further load of shock to the nervous system.

How can you tell if a therapy is working?

With regards to assessing if a trauma therapy has been helpful, it is important to consider the long term affects in one's life. After doing the therapy work, are you calmer, better regulated in your nervous system? Are your relationships more stable? Are your personal boundaries better? Is your life happier and more fulfilled? Having an intense experience, whether induced by the use of drugs, plant medicine, cathartic therapy does not indicate recovery. Remembering things that happened to you a long time ago that were distressing is not healing. Trauma is a condition that exists in the present moment functioning of your body/mind/emotions. You do not have to go back to the past to heal it. The healing happens right here in the present moment by regulating your nervous system and your 'affect'. Which means regulating your emotional and behavioural responses to challenging triggers. A sign of having healed your trauma is whether you have more 'capacity' in the present moment to difficult circumstances. Are you coping better with the challenges of life?

Trauma Vortex, Healing Vortex and Titration:

Dr Peter Levine talks about trauma having an energy like a great swirling vortex that can sweep you up and suck you down into it. Something will trigger you into activation and it begins spiralling and the nervous system will then begin sending out the alarm signals because the brain thinks that the original dangerous event is happening. If you carry on stimulating it, as you did with primal therapy, then you can get sucked all the way down into the trauma vortex and be re-traumatised. In this way, the trauma becomes more densely embedded as you are creating more and more neural pathways towards activation. 'Neurons that fire together, wire together'. Healing trauma is about creating new neural pathways. You can now begin to have a choice as to how you respond to your triggers. For this reason, it is not necessary to dig up all the old memories to heal trauma. It is not about remembering and getting endlessly activated into all the old pain. You can touch in on a memory as a point of activation of the pain, but then it is handed over to the Healing Vortex.

Alongside the Trauma Vortex is the Healing Vortex. So, when you approach your trauma with the intention of healing it, you bring a conscious awareness to it. This is your Healing Vortex. The intention is to heal. The first step is to become conscious. You need to begin to observe yourself as to witness your experience in the present moment. Do not just be driven by your activation levels. Imagine the Healing Vortex as running alongside the Trauma Vortex. It is driven by the conscious intention to heal. The Trauma Vortex needs to be activated. You now stay with your consciousness on the level of low activation only, not plunge into the depths of the spiral, which is a high level of activation. The Healing Vortex is moving in the opposite direction to the Trauma Vortex, so as one piece of activation spirals around, the Healing Vortex will pick it up and move it back in the other direction to be healed. This process is known as Titration.

Babette Rothschild talks about Titration with a different metaphor. She describes the trauma as being a bottle of Coke that has been really shaken up. The Healing Vortex is taking the top off the bottle without spilling the contents. Titration is turning the lid one little half turn at a time in order to let a little of the fizz out of the bottle. So, on the one hand, you have the activation of the trauma and on the other hand, healing happens through conscious intention. This conscious intention needs to be supported by a feeling of safety, otherwise, if you don't feel safe, you are never going to get the top off that bottle of fizzy coke.

Dr Peter Levine, who has created Somatic Experiencing as an important methodology for healing trauma also talks about Titration as being a process whereby you can touch into the difficult experience without becoming overwhelmed by it. You are taking a very small dose of the pain to become conscious of it and then you are moving away from it again (hence moving from the Trauma Vortex to the Healing Vortex). When you have tolerated or titrated the amount of bearable pain, then you move or pendulate away from it to a place where you feel 'resourced' or 'comfortable'. The healing process is brought about by moving between these two poles of experience. This movement is rhythmical and is patterned on the natural rhythm of the body of expansion and contraction. Everything in the body is always changing and experiences ebb and flow. When you are traumatised, it often feels like you are totally stuck in the pain, so if you can create a flow between these two poles, then you are moving out of the feeling of stuckness, which in itself can be very empowering.

Learning to notice and monitor your activation will help you to heal. You can start this process as soon as you understand about it.

Monitoring Your Activation:

Activation happens when you are triggered by some kind of sensory information which reminds you of the original traumatising event. Once you are triggered, the reptilian brain is acting as if that trigger is actually the real, life-threatening event.

It is important that you are able to be aware of whether you are activated or not. Activation can be in either direction. You can become very anxious or angry and agitated, or you can become frozen, numb, detached, spaced out. It is as if you are not really 'present' or in your body. You may also have an increase in other symptoms that you suffer from. You may experience more pain or panic. You might be tearful or your sensory awareness increases. You may be compulsively going into your coping mechanisms, taking a drink or a cigarette or some other displacement activity. Your body temperature may be unstable, becoming too hot or cold. In order to heal it is important to get into the habit of noticing the activation and giving it a number on a scale of 1–10. Set yourself a target of bringing it down as low as possible through resourcing yourself. To help you to be able to keep a record of how your Activation Levels are changing, we have listed some of the key markers in Chapter 4 for you to keep track of them over time.

Creating a 'felt sense' of safety is a fundamental step in healing trauma. Once you can begin to do this, you can gradually build on it and gain more control in your nervous system.

Safety in Healing Trauma:

Traumatisation happens to us in a situation where we are profoundly unsafe. It is an extreme experience of feeling that we are going to die at any moment. We may not be literally thinking that, but our nervous system is firing off as if this is a reality. Ongoing anxiety, anger and depression are all expressions of a nervous system in distress.

One of the foundation stones of healing trauma is through creating resources in your life. A process referred to as resourcing.

Feelings of hopelessness and overwhelm are the final attempts by the nervous system to protect you by causing you to conserve core energy by doing nothing except collapsing.

Life becomes very compromised and limited when you are continually in a state of activation. To prevent continual activation and to heal trauma, creating a feeling of safety is the number one step to take. This is something that you have to consciously intend and do on a continual basis. It may go against the grain of traditional behaviour because we are taught not to take care of ourselves, to work hard to earn money, to put others first. To be serious, to get a job, and not be selfish. You are going to have to let go of all those ideas. That is the way that the frontal cortex puts a spanner in the works of the reptilian brain.

You have to create Safety in your life. I will say that again. SAFETY IS YOUR PRIORITY

When you can begin to feel safe, then the amygdala will stop sending out the danger signals. If you push yourself into situations where you don't feel safe, where you feel more exhausted, more threatened, more overwhelmed, then the Trauma Spiral will deepen and you will be sucked down into it.

A feeling of safety is a somatic experience. You have to have the sensation of safety in your body. You have to relish it, enjoy it, savour it. Indulge it. It is a luscious feeling. When you can get that somatic feeling of safety in the body you will begin to heal.

Creating safety may be a challenging or difficult issue. It really depends on who you are, what has happened, and what your present environment is.

Creating safety might take a few easy steps or it may be that you are in an ongoing unsafe situation, and you have to strengthen your boundaries in order to create safety. We will come to that later. Here I am talking about creating in the moment , the felt sense of safety in the body. Along with the feeling of safety comes the feeling of comfort. Your nervous system cannot be feeling that you are about to die if you are feeling safe and comfortable. These feelings need to be SENSATIONS in the body. They are the Felt Sense.

Resourcing as a Way of Creating Safety:

Resourcing is a means of creating a sense of well-being, comfort and safety. **It is choosing to do things which support and nourish you, rather than endlessly being driven by your trauma reactions.** If you have spent a lifetime of not being resourced and have had, like me, a lifetime of feeling starved and simply there not being time for you or consideration for you, then now is the time to say **'ENOUGH'. It is my time now'.**

> *"During this process, I was very pleased with myself as I realised how many amazing resources I do actually have access to, gaining clarity of how the nervous system gets dis-regulated really helped me to understand when and how to apply these resources too."* Dr Marion Bevington

If you are serious about healing, you are going to have to spend a lot of time taking care of yourself and building your resources. When you are well resourced, then your primitive nervous system, the reptilian brain, is enabled to turn off the alarm signals that shout, 'danger, danger' and your activation levels will drop. We **CAN** heal from very traumatic events. It doesn't mean that what happened goes away and that there aren't feelings of regret, sadness, or anger but it does mean that we are no longer activated by those feelings in a fight-or-flight or collapse reaction. The experience that caused us to become traumatised has now been processed by the hippocampus and filed away as memories that are in the past, rather than fragments of 'undigested' memories that feel as if they are happening in the present moment.

So, what is a resource?

A resource can be anything that helps you feel good. Even having a cigarette or a drink can be a resource although this is not advisable because these activities are not beneficial to your overall health and lead eventually to other equally serious health problems. They are also highly addictive behaviours.

Addiction is a result of trauma according to Dr Gabor Mate, and addictions of any kind help to soothe the pain of the trauma by triggering dopamine, a neurotransmitter associated with pleasure. So, in a way, addiction is a form of a resourcing behaviour but with negative consequences, and thus not inherently healing.

Even the medical profession tries to 'resource' you when they give pharmaceutical drugs for managing depression and anxiety, but, again, these can be very addictive and, in the end, cause more problems. Equally, addictive behavior and the pharmaceutical approach tend to numb awareness as to the root problem of suffering. They both disempower you from initiating the healing vortex. In order to heal from trauma, you need to be in your power, creating healthy, life-affirming resources that will truly nourish you and help you move forward in your healing. You can only do this from a fully resourced body.

Trauma is a physical problem. It can only be healed through the body, through physical experiences. Trauma is a feeling that the body is about to perish. You change this feeling in your body to one of comfort and well being. This is being resourced.

When the body is resourced, it feeds information that all is well back to the primitive nervous system, the reptilian brain, and the panic turns off.

Let's explore what kinds of resources there are. Which are the ones that you like to do - or did like to do before you were traumatised or unwell?

Activities and Being in Nature:

A resource should ideally be something that physically gives you a sense of well-being in your body. It should be a physical activity of some kind. It can be walking, swimming dancing or any other relaxed activity. Yoga, pilates, tai chi, swimming or rowing are all examples. The list is long according to your personal preferences. Gardening is my favourite. I feel so at peace in a garden; nourished by the sounds of the birds and bees, and the scent of the flowers, the sun on my face, or a soft breeze gently caressing my skin. Walking and being in nature is a powerful healer for most people and, as a child, it was the resource that allowed me to survive when I felt so alone. I was able to be in nature and to be at peace. Where in nature do you like to be? It could be a local park or somewhere further out in the countryside. It could be something even wilder and more rugged. However, take care not to do anything too strenuous or challenging when in the early stages of healing. Be gentle with yourself. Simply sitting under a tree with your back against the trunk is calming. You can communicate with the tree. Listen to it. Let is speak to you.

Movement:

Any number of these kinds of activities are resourcing. Movement activities, in particular, are good, especially if you tend to suffer from overwhelm, because they will help you to unfreeze the energy that gets stuck in the body in trauma. The movement needs to be gentle, not aerobic. Strong movement that stimulates a high heart rate can lead to activation which is what we want to avoid. All resources should be un-activating, so if there is anything that you would choose that has a memory or trigger attached to it, then it is best to avoid it for the moment. If you do an activity that triggers you into a bad memory or to experience an activation, then stop doing that exercise for the time being until you are more healed and resilient.

When you are doing these activities, you should notice how it feels in the body. Where can you experience the sensation of comfort or well-being in your body?

Be body aware and conscious of sensation when you are doing things. Feel your feet on the ground, or even take time to go barefoot on the earth.

'Earthing' – walking barefoot on the earth - also helps you to discharge electromagnetism from your body which will help you to feel more refreshed and alive.

Other Sensory Experiences as Resources:

Other resourcing activities are listening to music or going to the theatre, or even joining a choir or a drama club. Moving the body and expressing through the voice is very powerful and healing. It may sometimes bring up emotions which were locked. Just be aware of this and know that it will pass.

Trauma is being stuck in the past. The present moment is now, and now is when you are safe and well.

Emotions need to flow and they will not harm you.

What is it that you used to do that you loved to do? Bring that activity back and re-establish it in your life. You might have to do it in baby steps at first, but slowly build up your engagement in that activity. Maybe painting or drawing or craftwork of some kind? Perhaps pottery, sculpture, or wood carving. All these activities are very relaxing and help the creative process. They will give you a better feeling about yourself, be in the present moment, and help you to come alive again.

Meditation:

Meditation is very good as a calming activity that soothes you, body and soul. It also helps you learn to be mindful, and you can then apply mindfulness to everything that you do. Mindfulness brings you into the present moment. Choose a meditation technique that brings you into an awareness of comfort in the body; something that is grounding. Don't do anything that encourages you to be out of your body. This is not the time to aim for enlightenment. The attainment of enlightenment is a pursuit for a healthy, strong, conscious person with a developed ego who has a daily practice of being anchored in the body.

Meditation techniques that aim to take you out of the body when you are not solidly grounded, and when you have a lot of trauma activated in your system, can take you into realms of distress and disturbance.

If you find yourself getting ungrounded and lost in your emotional process, then stop meditating for the time being.

Another good practice is Yoga Nidra. This brings you into an awareness of your body and helps it to heal itself. Should you find that it causes you to have flashbacks, a revisitation of a traumatic event, then stop the practice for a little while until you have healed some more, before returning to it.

Eating:

Food can be a wonderful resource, especially when it is good nourishing food.

You may have lost the incentive to make food for yourself, but if you can, make yourself some really nice food. Food is nourishing on all levels but may be problematic for some people if they have eating disorders. If that is not the case for you, then take the time to prepare healthy, appealing, delicious food. Ensure that your meals are regular, and steer away from food that undermines your health such as those laden with bad hydrogenated fats or sugar. Avoid processed food. Eat an abundance of fresh fruit and vegetables, and, in particular, eat foods that support your adrenal system.

If you have been unwell for a long time with traumatic reactions, your adrenal glands could be very depleted. The continual flooding of adrenaline and cortisol in your body takes a lot of energy and nutrients so depletion is likely.

Also, ensure that you drink adequate fresh water and, preferably, some vegetable juices. Hydration is very important. Our body is around 60% water. It is necessary for good cell function, digestion, and to keep the body moving and detoxed. If possible get a good water filter. Charcoal blocks in a jug of water help to take unwanted chemicals out of the water, such as chlorine.

Bathing:

Having long hot baths with Epsom salts or some essential oils can be very relaxing. Make a ritual of it and pamper yourself. Take the time to be quiet and to just really give yourself all the time that you need. Also showering is good.

You can use the sensation of the shower on the skin to help you feel more connected to yourself.

When you have been very overwhelmed you can feel disconnected or numb in your body. For some people, there may be a feeling that their legs or arms are not really there or are hollow or empty.

When you are in the shower, focus the spray on each part of the body and say to yourself, 'this is my arm, hello arm'. 'This is my leg, hello leg'. Little by little you will begin to get back the sense of your body. You can also do this in the bath by speaking to each body part as you make contact with yourself when feeling the sensation of a sponge or flannel.

Sleeping:

For many people who are traumatised, sleeping is difficult. Good sleep is essential to health, and to be in bed before midnight allows your body to detox itself at a cellular level. When you are suffering from adrenal exhaustion, the tendency is to become awake later in the night and start to do things at that time even though you were tired earlier in the day.

Resist this tendency because it only deepens the cycle of exhaustion. Avoid stimulating activities late at night or taking any intoxicants, especially cigarettes or alcohol which affect blood sugar levels, causing them to drop whilst sleeping. This will later wake you up again after you have fallen asleep. Make a ritual of bedtime. Prepare yourself by gradually unwinding and making preparations for a good night's sleep. Ensure that your sleeping place is comfortable and feels like a safe place for you. If you do not feel safe, then have a lock on the door. Take time to check your room before getting into bed if you feel unsafe. Tell yourself that you are safe and even look under the bed to settle yourself and focus on the comfort that you can find in your body. Do some gentle stretches before bed. Make yourself warm and cosy; perhaps have a hot water bottle or a cuddly toy. If you have a tendency to wake up with bad dreams, write a notice and put it on the wall or somewhere where you can see it when you wake. Write on it, 'I am completely safe now, even though I just had a bad dream', or some other similar words that can soothe you. Do whatever is necessary for you to have a settled, enjoyable sleep.

You may be helped by listening to some relaxing music or 'white noise' or the sound of a gentle heartbeat. Another helpful aid is a sensory or gravity blanket that gently wraps itself around you and gives the feeling of human contact. CBD oil (Cannabidoil) also helps reduce stress and anxiety, and aids sleep. You can also drink herbal tea, such as chamomile or valerian. Make sure that your room is dark so that you can drop more easily into a deep sleep - unless you find that having a low light is more soothing for you.

If you tend to wake in the night, it is better to get up and have a soothing drink or do some gentle activity than lying for hours trying to go back to sleep.

Relaxation:

Relaxation is very important in healing from trauma. It is important to set time aside each day to just 'be'. Do make a space when you don't have to do anything at all. You may find it difficult at first to relax. Also, for some people when they have extreme trauma, they find that at the start of the relaxation process they begin to feel anxious and agitated. If this happens to you, know that with repeated practice, this will eventually stop. If it is happening, remind yourself that the past is over with and that you are now safe to relax. Booking yourself a weekly massage or craniosacral session will help you get more into your body in a safe and a relaxed way. Take time to explain to your therapist that you have been suffering from trauma and that you need to be in control of the session. It is important to feel safe. Choose a light massage rather than a deep tissue massage unless you are clear that a deep tissue massage will not overwhelm your body and stir up memories or pain that is activating. Listening to some quiet music or other quiet activity can also be relaxing. If you feel very tense or agitated, then a gentle walk will be a way to relax. It will help you release the tense energy whilst you observe nature or your surroundings as you walk.

Baby Steps:

It may be that you have felt so overwhelmed or phobic for so long that any of the things that I have described above are too difficult for you to do. In this case, it is important to take baby steps and to slowly build up your resources. One day at a time. One small activity at a time. Remember you are turning your life around. You are initiating the Healing Vortex. It is probably the most important task that you will ever do. Do it consciously, and, if possible, get some help.

Friends and Community:

Having social connections can be a great resource.

If we are traumatised we often become lonely and isolated. If we have never felt either safe or confident in our lives it may affect our ability to connect with others. Our sense of self-worth and self-esteem may have been undermined.

Often traumatised people carry a huge amount of shame. All this can be healed, but at the moment it may still be having an effect in these early stages.

It is important to rebuild your connections with a loving and supportive community.

A resourcing step is to look for a group activity such as a community garden, a social club, an art class, or something else you enjoy or have thought that one day you might like to do. Maybe there is an organisation that you would like to volunteer for that gives you a greater sense of purpose?

Trauma fractures our lives, mentally, emotionally and relationally. it causes us to numb ourselves. It tears our communities apart. 'Re-connecting' and 're-membering' are literally putting back these parts again; rebuilding our connections. We are strong together. We are safe and we can support each other. There may have been people in the past that did you harm, but this is not the case now. You can choose who you are going to connect with, and you can have a new awareness of what caused this to happen in the past. Now you have an understanding that is increasing on a daily basis, and you will learn how to establish boundaries that support your feeling of safety. Write a list of friends that you love and trust. Have the list available so that you can call them if you need them. Maybe you haven't been in touch for a very long time. Test the water and reach out to them. Write them a letter or make a call. Tell them if you can that you have been unable to be in touch but you would like to be again. Ask them if they can support you. Human beings need to be connected to each other. Isolation and aloneness are not good for anyone. We need each other, especially when we have been through such challenging circumstances and traumatised.

Tracking your recovery:

Resources need to be built on a daily basis, and implemented little by little; in this way, you will find that your life can gradually change. However, the changes may not be noticeable to you unless you keep some kind of record of how you were in the beginning and how you are now. It is important to have some way of tracking your improvement so that you don't feel despondent on those days when you feel like you are not making any progress. A diary is a good idea or a chart that you can easily mark on a daily basis.

Now you know about safety and how resourcing helps to create a 'felt sense' of security, you are well on the way to healing trauma. The more you take care of yourself in this way, the quicker you will heal. This is proven by the neurobiology.

Now that you know that you are not a bad person, just a traumatised person, you don't have to punish yourself by not taking care of yourself.

To heal yourself you have to create a feeling of safety in your body by taking care of yourself by doing pleasant things.

CHAPTER 4

Trauma Healing Exercises

These exercises have been extensively
practised by many of my clients and
students and have been found to be
extremely helpful in healing trauma.

In this chapter, we will explore exercises that will help you
feel resourced and enable you to gain a grounded,
connected feeling with your body. It will enable you to build
up body awareness and help to release stuck or frozen
trauma energies and somatic armouring.

*"One of the greatest resources I now use for
calming my nervous system is the Earth
herself. Either lying on the ground (sky bathing)
or holding pebbles can greatly discharge any
build-up of nervous energy. When I do this
during the night to help me fall back to sleep, I
almost always have a healing or prophetic
dream which helps in the process."*
Rachel Elnaugh

RESOURCING:

The first step in this process is to build a solid foundation of
resources.

Exercise 1

Planning or Visioning Your Resources:

Creating a map of possible resources is a good starting point. Getting a large piece of paper and some coloured pens or crayons is helpful. You don't have to be an artist and you don't have to be able to accurately represent things. A symbol or a word is sufficient, but if you can make it more picture-like, then do so. Take time to create a clear space where you know that you won't be disturbed. Make the space comfortable for yourself; sufficiently light and warm, at the right degree of comfort so that you can be relaxed. Settle yourself down with the sheet of paper and the crayons in front of you. Sit comfortably and be aware of your body making contact with the place that you are sitting. Take several deep breaths and allow your body to feel a little heavier and relax as you do so. Pick up a coloured crayon you are drawn to and like, and make a drawing or symbol of yourself at the centre of the paper. Make yourself as big as you can whilst leaving space for your resources to be drawn around you. Then, when you are happy with the drawing of yourself, allow an awareness of what you really like to do or did like to do, come to you. Find a place on the paper to draw that or make a symbol of it. Continue in this way until your self-image is completely surrounded by pictures or symbols of your resources.

This picture can be placed on the wall for you to see on a daily basis. If you want to keep it private, then put it away somewhere where you can easily access it on a daily basis. You will need to continually look at it in order to remind yourself. Now celebrate that you have created your resource plan. As you get new resources or new ideas for resources, you can add them to your plan. Take time out to do something nice for yourself and tell yourself 'well done'.

SOMATIC EXPERIENCING

Somatic Experiencing is about being in touch with your body and understanding how your experiences are 'embodied'. Trauma is healed by creating sensation in the body. When we have been very overwhelmed, we may lose connection with the body. Shock can cause us to dissociate so that we no longer are aware of our bodies. If we have been physically abused, it may be hard to be in the body since the body was unsafe. If this is the case for you, then just take this part slowly. Don't get frustrated if you cannot feel your body. Even a feeling of numbness is information. You may notice that you have no feeling in one part of your body and some feeling in another part of your body, or that you only have partial feeling somewhere. You may become aware that you have a 'split' between top and bottom or side to side of your body, or that you are all in your head. Whatever the distortion is, or the lack of feeling, this will gradually change. A fully embodied sense of self will come in time as you build a sense of safety and an awareness that the past is over and the present moment is all that there is.

Exercise 2

Somatic Experiencing

To do this exercise, find a space where you will not be disturbed and where you can be warm and comfortable.

Find a comfortable chair to sit in. Take a deep breath and allow your breath to flow out in a long out-breath. As you are doing this, allow your body to become heavier. Feel the out-breath blowing across your bottom lip. Do this about six times.

Now bring your attention to your feet on the ground. Notice what they feel like? On the next out-breath, allow them to be heavier and more in contact with the ground. What does the ground feel like? Notice it and analyse it. Is it hard or soft? Bumpy, smooth, prickly. It may sound silly, but go through all the possible sensations that your feet could be feeling in contact with the ground. Can you feel sensation all the way across your feet? Are there any places in your feet where you don't feel sensation? Is it the same on both feet? If it is not the same, what is the difference? What is the temperature like on your feet? Is it the same all the way over and under your feet? What else is there to notice about your feet?

Taking another long out-breath, become aware now of your thighs and bottom on the chair. What is the contact like? Can you feel yourself sitting there? Is there pressure? Are you comfortable? Are the pressure and contact the same all the way across your thighs and bottom? Is it the same on both sides? What is the temperature like in this area? Is it the same temperature as your feet? What else is there to be aware of in this area?

Now feel your back against the chair. Is your back in contact with the chair? What is the contact like? Can you feel it all the way up your back, or are there some gaps in the contact? Is it hard or soft or some other sensation? What is the temperature of your back? Is it the same as your thighs and bottom and the same as your feet? Or is it a different temperature?

Becoming aware of your shoulders. Are they touching the chair? If so, what do they feel like? What do your neck and head feel like? What temperature do you feel in these areas? Is it the same as your back? What do your arms feel like? Are they in contact with the chair or are they resting across your body? What temperature are they? Are they the same temperature and sensation, or different? In what way are they different?

Finally become aware of sensation down the front of your body. What are you feeling in this area? What is the temperature like here?

If you have been feeling cold in different parts of your body, take a blanket and make yourself cosy. Now notice where in your body do you feel comfortable? If you can find a place of comfort, settle your awareness into the comfort and allow yourself to relax into it. Take a breath and let yourself settle more deeply into the comfort. Allow your body to become a little heavier a little more relaxed. Remind yourself that you are completely safe right now.

Notice other sensations of comfort and well-being in your body. Allow them to spread as much as they want to. Continue to take some deep breaths and allow yourself to relax more fully into the comfort that you feel in your body. Remind yourself again that, in this moment, you are completely safe and the past is over and done with.

A Daily Practice:

It is good to spend time doing this every day and, in fact, whenever you are sitting down. Make it a habit to check out your somatic awareness. You don't always have to go into such detail, but you can notice your basic contact and seek out any sensations of comfort in your body. Likewise, when standing somewhere, you can notice the contact of your feet on the ground I tend to do this to relax quite frequently throughout the day. Also, if I am anxious about something, I will make a point of tuning into my somatic awareness. After the car accidents, when I was frightened of driving, I used to practice this as I was driving. It would calm me down and help to diminish the fear.

As you get more used to doing this, and finding more comfort in your body, then you can take your awareness deeper, so that it is not just your surface contact that you are feeling. You can get a sense of what else is going on. You may notice all kinds of sensations. Eventually, you can listen and feel for how you are embodying various emotional states that you are feeling, remembering to come back all the time to the resourced comfortable state.

In this way, you can begin to pendulate and titrate your experience.

You can start by noticing the emotion that you are feeling. Once you have become aware of this, you can notice what your body is doing in the area where you are feeling the emotion. For instance, if you feel sadness, where are you feeling the sadness? Which part of your body? Maybe it is in your chest, or your heart. Perhaps it is in your throat? Maybe it is in your eyes? Notice what this feels like? What is happening physically in these parts of the body? Spend a moment to notice this, but don't get sucked into it. Now move away from the feeling. Move to a feeling of comfort in your body. Where do you feel this? What does the comfort feel like? Allow it to expand. When this is well established, you can move back to the feeling of sadness and notice what that is like. What is your body doing now? How does the sad place feel? What has changed?

Continue alternating between the two feelings, that of the comfort and the sadness. Witness the changes that are happening. This is the way to begin to heal the trauma. You are freeing up the frozen trauma energies and stuck feelings in the body. You are titrating (staying with a feeling to explore it and building up a tolerance for the discomfort) and pendulating (moving away from the feeling when it is too uncomfortable or before it gets overwhelming) and resourcing (staying present in a safe way to your experience through a feeling of comfort so that the trauma can heal).

Going deeper with somatic experiencing and working with feelings of numbness or dissociation:

It may be that you find this exercise very difficult and that you are not comfortable trying to get in touch with your body. If this is the case, then take it very slowly.

Working slowly is good and yields powerful healing results.

If you have been physically abused, you may not like tuning into your body very much. Also, if you are really badly traumatised you may be very dissociated. You may not be aware of the level or nuances of your dissociation. This can be gradually tracked over time. Do you feel that you are not in your body? Or are you out of your body a long way? Or are you partially out of your body? Are you to the left or right of your body? Are you in your arms but not your legs for instance? This is something that you can explore very gently. Do not force yourself. You may blame yourself for 'not being present' or feel that you are 'lazy' or 'disconnected'. The first step here is to begin to build compassion for yourself and to understand that you have had no choice in this. It is a result of your reptilian brain protecting you at a time when you really were in a life and death situation, a perceived life and death situation, or when you were witnessing someone else in that situation.

Parasympathetic shock or dissociation happens as a result of overwhelming life-threatening circumstances. It is the nervous system's way of disconnecting you from the intense suffering of such an experience. As explained earlier, it is the way that the reptilian brain makes a last desperate attempt to protect you. Remember the way that the antelope drops, apparently dead to the ground, just as the lion is catching it. Well if you are dissociating, it is because you are stuck in this part of the nervous system defence cycle. Your reptilian brain is still acting as if you are in danger. When it first put you in this state, it saved your life, but now it is stuck in the cycle and it may not be serving you any longer. It may be affecting your life so that you are not able to direct it meaningfully. It may be blocking you from being 'present' in relationships. It can leave you with a tendency to 'opt-out' of life whenever you get triggered by something. This can lead you to be critical or unkind to yourself, or ashamed of yourself.

The first step in healing this is what might be a challenging step to become aware of your level of dissociation and very gently bring more conscious awareness to that experience. It will gradually change and it is important to notice this as it happens.

Take it very slowly so that you can connect the dots of what has happened to you. In this way, you can unravel the trauma safely.

Notice when you start to do the somatic experiencing exercise whether you can feel parts of your body, or whether there are gaps in your awareness. Where are the gaps and what do they feel like? If you feel as if you are not in your body, then where are you in relation to your body? How far out are you?

Do not try to make yourself come back. This is about witnessing, not forcing.

Begin to track your tendency to lift out of your body. How often does it happen and under what circumstances? Learn to be able to notice if you spend lots of time dissociated and if there are varying degrees of it. What kinds of situations cause you to dissociate? Are there particular places which cause it to happen? Do certain people trigger it? Are there memories that cause it to happen? Or being in a group? Or being alone? Are there certain smells, or textures or colours that trigger it?

Before you start working too intensely on this, find something that can really resource you. It may be that you can find a feeling of comfort in your body, but this may be hard if you are completely numb or dissociated. In this instance, go to your map of resources and see if there is something else to resource you. It might be a picture, or a crystal, or some music. It might be actually getting up and moving your body. Notice what helps that dissociative feeling to change.

Does the tendency to dissociate change as you begin to titrate the experience with a sense of comfort? If you are not easily able to do this then track carefully through your body for a feeling of comfort anywhere. Is there a sense of comfort somewhere, even if it is only the tip of your finger? Is the feeling of comfort simply an absence of numbness or pain? This is something that may take time to build up.

Don't be disheartened or stressed by this. It is fine if it takes a while. Don't give up. It will change. If you can move anywhere in your body between two different feelings, it means that you are NOT STUCK and that you are making progress. Be compassionate, it also means that you have had a lot of trauma, and that you need to take a lot of care and time to heal yourself. You will achieve this if you keep practising. It may be that it would be helpful to seek some expert help with this. Finding a good somatic experiencing practitioner or a body-based psychotherapist can provide the additional experience of safety that will help you move out of this dissociative frozen state.

Becoming Embodied:

The aim of the somatic experiencing exercises are that eventually, you build a feeling of being fully embodied. Sometimes this can take years to achieve, sometimes a lifetime. We may gradually come into our bodies in 'fits' and 'starts'. A little bit at a time, on each turn of the healing vortex, we find a little more embodiment.

When you are not fully embodied, it is harder to engage with life and to feel fully 'present' energetically. It is hard to feel fully in your power when 'disembodied'.

Sometimes, if you are really finding it difficult to get any sense of your body, it is easier to start resourcing from a place that is outside of the body. Your imagination is very powerful in helping you to do this, which leads us to the next exercise.

Exercise 3

Visualising a Place where you Feel Good

If it is altogether too difficult to feel into your body, can you think of an activity that you like to do or a place that you enjoy being in? Whatever you choose has to be free from any activating memory or association. So, don't imagine any places that are linked with any kind of bad or negative experience. Do not bring any people into your imaginary situation unless you are 100% confident in your feelings of safety and comfort with them.

Imaginary situations can be deeply healing and lead to very positive and successful outcomes. The effects of an imaginary positive experience on your nervous system are as powerful as if they were actually happening. The brain believes whatever you create in the imagination, and will send the appropriate signals, in the form of neurotransmitters, to the body to tell it to relax or be activated. For this reason, the process of imagining is a powerful tool. It is a step towards building more sensory awareness and safety in the body. Do not worry whether you can clearly see images or pictures in this imaginary exercise. Some people can and some can't. If like me, you can't see them, then just describe them to yourself with words.

To start this exercise, find a quiet, safe, and comfortable place where you won't be disturbed. Make sure that you are cosy. If you like, you can light a candle and burn some incense. Set the intention to have a healing experience. Settle yourself in a chair in a comfortable position. Take a breath and a long out-breath, blowing the air over your bottom lip. Do this about six times. Imagine your body becoming heavier and more relaxed.

Bring to mind a place of peace. Perhaps it is a special place in nature where that you have enjoyed being in the past or an idyllic scene you create. Imagine that place now. Imagine yourself in the place. See yourself there. Where are you exactly? Are you sitting or standing, walking or doing some other activity? What does it look like? Slowly bring into your mind all the things about it that you remember or like, trees, flowers, any buildings or fences or special features. What is the weather like? Can you feel it? Feel the breeze on your face or sunshine on your skin. What sounds are you hearing? Notice them each individually. Are there particular bird calls that you recognise? Can you hear the wind? Do you hear the sounds of the ocean or the trickling of a stream? Do you hear the rushing noise of a waterfall? The sounds of some an animal? Perhaps there are other sounds that you like which are soothing to you? What is the quality of the light like? Is it bright and sunny? Or cloudy? Are the clouds moving, creating patches of dark and light? Or is it overcast? What is the feel of the atmosphere? Give yourself permission to relax here. You know that it is a special place for you. You have a good connection with it.

You are entirely safe. Stay there and enjoy it for as long as you like. You can return to this place in your imagination whenever you want to. As you spend a while in this imaginary place, become aware of your body. How is it feeling now? Be aware of any sensation of comfort in your body. Once you notice a feeling of comfort in your body, allow yourself to settle into it a little more.

What if it is unsafe to relax?

For some people, a feeling of relaxation can trigger a feeling of danger. They may start to get agitated as a result of relaxing. It can also be that they don't 'deserve' to relax. Should you get anxious or agitated every time you begin to relax, know that this can be normal. You need to work on this very slowly. When you get to the edge of that feeling of discomfort, then it is helpful to actually get up and move your body around. Open your eyes and look at something that is soothing. Remind yourself that you are safe and well in this moment and that the feeling of agitation comes from a time when you were not safe. Take time to deliberately explore the room that you are in. Look–in every nook and cranny. You may know logically that it is safe, but we are dealing here with your primitive brain which is not switching off the danger signals, so you need to reassure it by checking things out. You can even go to the door, open it, and step outside. Notice if the feelings of agitation calm as you do this.

Repeat this exercise each time you begin to get agitated when relaxing. Notice the process that is happening and reassure yourself each time with compassion.

Boundaries:

Boundaries are an important part of life and are both a physical and a psychological construct. They give a sense of self. They keep us safe. We can feel where we are in relationship with another human being. This is mine and that is yours. They show us where we need to take responsibility and where others are responsible.

Boundaries need to be clear and strong yet have a little 'give' in them when necessary.

When you have had events in your life where you have been very overwhelmed and been left with your nervous system continually pumping out cortisol and adrenaline, you may feel unsafe most of the time. If you have been abused as a child or had a very difficult and troubling marriage, or even a business partnership or other relationship where your boundaries have been ignored, then now is the time to implement them.

This is another exercise of the imagination. This time you are also setting an intention. What do you want in your life? What is acceptable to you? Are there things that you have allowed to happen that make you unhappy. Now is the time to change that. What are they? Be clear that you will no longer tolerate them in your life. It might be frightening to make this public to other people at this point. The first step is to do it privately for yourself. You will sense how this feels and then you can implement it with others when you feel strong. You are gradually building a strong boundary where there wasn't one. This may be one of many that you need to put in place.

As you proceed, you can begin to be more conscious of these boundaries and implement them in your life. You may have someone seriously challenging them. Are you, for instance, in a divorce process or some other arbitration process? Are you having a difficult relationship with a parent, boss, or child? Or some other person who is in 'authority'? Take courage. You can have clear and strong boundaries. You have certain inalienable rights as a human being that no one is allowed to transgress. Creating a clear boundaries will help you be in your power.

When you have never had a boundary, it may be difficult to hold it in place in a way that is solid yet also a little flexible when need be. You might just want to hide forever behind that boundary thus making it difficult to negotiate important situations. If you have never have never had good boundaries modelled for you it might take a lot of practice to know how to do it. It can be scary, especially if you have never been allowed to say 'NO".

For this reason, I suggest that you do the following exercise. You can review it over time and repeat it as you build the skill and apply it in your life.

The exercises to develop boundaries, and to feel somatically where boundaries have been crossed, for me, those exercises were life-changing.   Julia Pennington

Exercise 4

Boundaries

First of all, make yourself as comfortable and relaxed as you can. Be in a place where you are not going to be disturbed. Set the intention: 'I am consciously creating my boundaries to protect myself from interference and invasion. I have a right to do this. It is my life.'

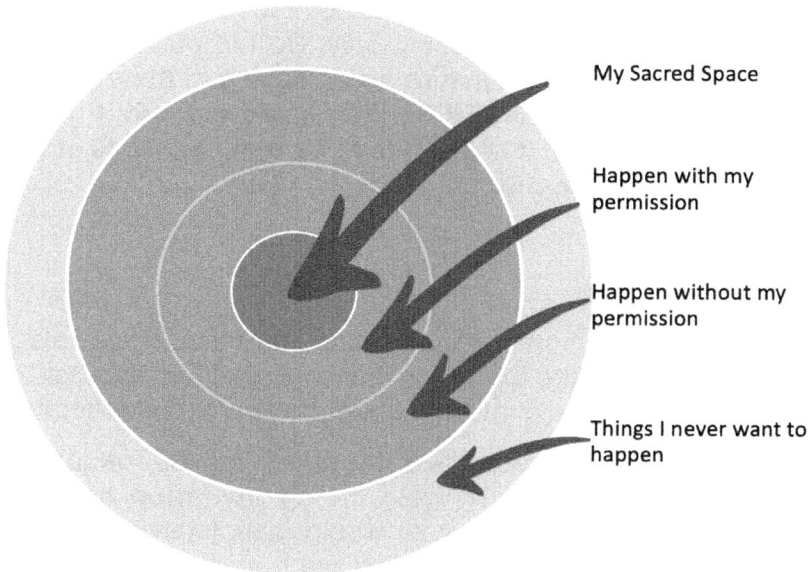

My Sacred Space

Happen with my permission

Happen without my permission

Things I never want to happen

You can either use the template of the three circles, or simply draw them on a big sheet of paper. You can use coloured pens again if you like. The three circles are one inside the other.

Inner Circle:

This inner circle represents your most sacred, intimate, and personal space.

In the centre you place yourself. You can draw either a symbol of yourself or a picture. Now think about what you would be comfortable to share this intimate space with. This can be a person, a pet, a situation. It may be that you would not allow anything into this space apart from yourself - or you might allow a child or partner in this space.

Now draw, write, or put symbols in that inner circle with yourself. Put anything that you choose to allow into your life with your absolute permission only. Do not put anything in that you feel remotely unsure about having in there. This is your sacred space and NOTHING is allowed into it unless you expressly want it to be. It may be that nothing is in that circle. That is your choice.

Second Circle:

In this second circle that is around the inner circle, place things, represented by using either a picture, symbol, or word, that you would invite in under certain circumstances.

Things that you would like to have, maybe people or situations that you would welcome **by invitation only**. Do not include things that you would absolutely not want. These are things that you might want sometimes, but not other times. Like a certain person that would be welcome sometimes but not other times. You give yourself permission to choose in the moment. It would still be your decision to allow it in according to how you are feeling at the time.

Third Circle:

In this third circle, which is the outer one, include things that you might occasionally allow in, but that you are not too sure about. Things that you haven't quite made up your mind about whether you enjoy it or whether you are entirely safe with. Things that you are perhaps exploring, but you are not going to allow to come too close to you until you have made up your mind about them.

Outside the Final Circle:

In this outside area, perhaps choosing a red pen or crayon, put things that you would **NEVER, UNDER ANY CIRCUMSTANCES,** allow into your life. This area represents an absolute **NO**. These would include situations that you find profoundly unsafe or people that have harmed you. Or they are things that you really do not enjoy at all.

The great teaching in this exercise was that boundaries can be fluid and flexible rather than rigid and fear-based"
Rachel Elnaugh

Now that you have finished doing your circles, notice how you are feeling in your body. Do you feel safe and good, or are you feeling activated? If you are activated, how activated are you on a scale of 1 – 10? Perhaps you can make a note of this on your activation chart or in your diary.

Here are some examples of the key activation markers for you to score:

Marker 1:   10 = Feeling sociable and wanting to relate to other people.
Or: 1 = Feeling withdrawn and wanting to avoid people.

Marker 2:   10 = Feeling calm and able to deal with challenging situations
Or: 1 = Feeling agitated, anxious and unable to cope with anything

Marker 3:   10 = Feeling positive and creative
Or: 1 = Feeling depressed, flat, numb and disinterested in everything.

Marker 4:   10 = Feeling energised and wanting to be engaged in life.
Or: 1 = Feeling no energy and can't be bothered with doing anything.

Marker 5:   10 = Feeling your mind is clear and you can solve problems
Or: 1 = Feeling woolly headed, spaced out and can't add up numbers or form a sentence clearly.

Marker 6:   10 = Feeling excitement for the day ahead
Or: 1 = Feeling dread or disinterest for the day ahead.

Marker 7:   10 = Feeling embodied, strong, healthy and vibrant.
Or: 1 = Feeling disconnected physically, weak, unwell.

Marker 8.   10 = Feeling you want to take care of yourself and make your home nice.
Or: 1 = Feeling no interest in self care or home making.

Marker 9:   10 = Feeling able to maintain a good balanced routine which supports your day.
Or: 1 = Having no routine and being completely chaotic.

Marker 10: 10 = Sleeping well and nourishing yourself.
Or: 1 = Not sleeping well and living on junk food.

How to define "Activation" - Are you really 'present' or in your body?

Do you feel anxious, angry, agitated, frozen, numb, detached, spaced out.

Can you sense any pain, panic, tearful, clenched, fearful of your sensory awareness increases.

Compulsively going to your coping mechanisms like drink, a cigarette or some other displacement activity.

Are you feeling too hot or cold.

By keeping a diary of your scores, you will get into the habit of noticing the activation and giving it a number on a scale of 1–10, set yourself a target of bringing it down as low as possible through resourcing yourself and following the Monthly program detailed in chapter 7.

Add up the scores from Marker 1 - 10 and keep a record of total scores.   The higher the scores, the greater your improvement.

Now congratulate yourself on completing the task and go and do something nice for yourself that is resourcing. This is good and powerful work that you have done

Exercise 5

Physically implementing your circles:

This is a further exercise that builds on the work you did with the drawing of the circles. Do not do it on the same day. Leave a little time so that the previous work can be integrated. Perhaps a couple of days. Notice how the other exercise with the circles has brought more awareness to you about what kind of boundaries you have and where you need to improve them.

With this exercise, please again start the work when you are comfortable and resourced. Be in a room or somewhere you will not be disturbed. You will need a larger space to lay the circles out on the floor. You will also need some objects, some cushions, or something to mark the circles. You need enough objects to make the three circles as large as they need to be. Now construct the three circles by laying out the objects in three circles on the floor.

When the set-up of the circles is completed, prepare yourself to do the exercise. Take a moment to ground yourself. Take a breath and then a long out-breath. Now step into the centre of the inner circle. This is your inner circle - your sacred, private space. Notice in your body what it feels like to be in the centre of those three circles. Take a number of breaths with long out-breaths. Feel your feet on the ground. Now notice any sensations in your body. What are you feeling in this moment? You may feel all kinds of physical sensations. It could be tension somewhere in your limbs or diaphragm. It could be tingling. It could be a feeling of anxiety or a sense of relief. Whatever the sensation, it is telling you something about what it feels like to be in your sacred space.

Take a moment to tell yourself that you are entirely safe and that the past is over with. Tell yourself **'this is my safe place and no one can enter.'** Nothing is allowed in here unless you expressly want it in. You are totally in control. Notice how this feels in your body. If you feel activated, how activated are you? You may need to titrate this activation with some resourcing. Search for some pleasant sensation in your body or move your eyes around the room and see what is comforting around you. Once you have found this, you can pendulate this pleasant sensation with any feelings of activation that you may feel. You may need to slow down or pause. If this exercise feels too intense, you can stop it and continue again on a different day.

When you are sufficiently calm and resourced, and you have noticed all the information that your body is showing you, take a breath and then a long out-breath and step into the second circle. Say to yourself, **'This is my second circle and I only allow things in here by invitation.** Again, check how this feels in your body. What is happening in your body? What subtle sensations are you aware of? Do you need to resource yourself again? If so, follow the resourcing process you did previously. Again, it is okay to stop if too many feelings and sensations are coming up for you, and you are beginning to feel overwhelmed. You can come back to this exercise. If you felt grounded in the second circle and noticed everything that your body had brought up to show you, then you can move into the third circle.

Take a breath and a long out-breath, step into your outer circle and see how this feels. Say,

'I will allow some things in here that I am are unclear about but this is as far as they will go.'

Check into your body and feel what is happening. Are you activated or resourced? What sensations do you notice? Do you need to resource yourself further? Do you need to take a pause or a break?

Now it is a time to consider the space outside the circles. Take a breath and a long out-breath. **Do not go over the line to the outer circle**. Be aware of your feet on the ground and the connection with the earth. When it feels strong, look outside the final circle line and say.

'Out there are the things that I never want in-my life and they will NEVER CROSS MY BOUNDARY UNDER ANY CIRCUMSTANCE.'

Feel this very clearly in your body and notice what happens. What subtle feelings and sensations are going on? Is there emotion? Is there sensation? How is it different or the same as what you felt in the inner circles? Be as aware as you can be and notice as much as possible. Do you feel strong, resourced, and confident or do you feel activated? If activated, how activated? If you are very activated, you may need to resource yourself again using the method that you did earlier.

If you need to stop and come back to the exercise on another day, it is okay to do this.

Well done with this exercise! Please note your experience of doing this exercise in your diary or your activation chart.

You may do this exercise as many times as you like. You can also bring it into your daily life by imagining it when necessary. When you are faced with difficult situations, imagine yourself in the centre of your circle. You can bring the awareness of your circles into every life choice that you make. As you are making the decision you can say to yourself.

'Where am I going to allow this experience in my life? Which of my boundaries is it going to cross? How much do I invite it in?'

When you have completed this exercise and it feels powerful and strong in your life, you can move on to the next one.

"The Boundaries exercise was such a profound process for me - I realised I do not have access to, nor clarity about, my own sacred space; it was like I have no right to something that is not defined and distributed by some external authority... not knowing what was present in my sacred space, I found the writing process almost impossible and then when I had to step into this space I felt very scared, exposed, and dissociated very easily. Being violated seemed like a normal part of life, so I was shocked by this finding, but it revealed so much about my own unhealthy attachments to what others needed to be happy around me - I had made it both my responsibility to appease others as soon as my overly sensitive "they are getting upset" radar was triggered... And I also realised how much deeply buried resentment I had toward others because they always seemed to absorb all of my attention... Disrupting this process left me feeling disconnected from others... I am still working on allowing my own inner connection, to me and my own inner authority, to develop and grow"
Dr, Marion Bevington

Exercise 6

Saying 'NO'

Why are we not able to say 'No' to bad things happening?

Traumatic situations are sometimes big and bad but they can also be subtle, and happen when we are very tiny. For instance, if our mother, although really loving us, was too deeply stressed to really give us the kind of parenting that we needed, we may have felt unlovable because we didn't have her full attention. We were too little and vulnerable to have been able to say 'no' I don't feel loved when you are not noticing me, please pay me attention.

Because we felt insecure in our Mother's love we may not have pushed for what we needed. We may have compromised our needs in order to feel more secure. We may have behaved in an inauthentic way in order to 'please' our distracted Mother. This may have compromised the developing circuitry of our brain, consequently inhibiting our ability to feel motivated and happy, or 'present' and focus on what was in front of us. This left a deep pain at a soul level which is now expressed as trauma in our nervous system.

If our life was suddenly turned over by a life-threatening event, such as an accident, war, or a natural disaster, the event may have happened so quickly that again we were unable to say 'NO" and protect our self.

If the traumatic experience, slowly, insidiously eroded away our life in some way, like a dark cloud creeping over us - such as being in a long term abusive relationship or living under the tyranny of a dictatorship - we may have slowly crumbled and never been able to say 'NO'. Or, if our life was always bad and we always had the feeling that we might die, saying 'NO" was not an option.

Either way, the traumatising events played out. These events were too dire, too fraught with emergency or anxiety to put the brakes on. We were not able to stop them or say 'NO' to them. We can be thankful however that in each time, our nervous system took over in a primitive response for our core survival. It is fortunate, in all those circumstances, that our primitive brain was able to protect us by putting us into 'fight-or-flight' or 'parasympathetic shock'.

If after being put into that parasympathetic activation, we were unable to discharge that energy, then we would have been left traumatised.

And being traumatised means that we have become disconnected from our self and our present needs. Our brain may have shrunk, and we may have lost the ability to be self-reflective, to be able to see what is truly happening now. Our perceptions may have become distorted. The part of the brain responsible for memory may be compromised and stuck. We will be stuck in the past with tunnel vision. We will still be fearful of those past events as if they were still happening now. They may come to us in dreams or in visual or emotional flashbacks. We will be feeling the pain of something that happened to us a very long time ago. OR, we may have been numbed completely by the activation of the primitive brain so that we simply don't feel anything anymore. We may live in our heads and think life is just fine but on an inner level, we may be unconsciously feeling hollow. If you have lost your connections and relations, you may not have any way of sharing that painful feeling.

Healing trauma is about RE-CONNECTING. It is about getting our power back. It is about connecting back to our core life force energy and feeling happy, enlivened, and even joyous.

The first step to healing this trauma is to know that life is different now. **The past is over.** Even if you still have difficult circumstances in your life, you are now empowered to make choices and changes that are bringing you profound healing and relief.

Are you now ready and willing to commit 100% to your healing? When we commit without reservation, all things are possible.

In order to bring your experience of the traumatic event in the past up to date, and rebuild those places where your boundaries were ruptured, learning to say 'NO' is an important step. The exercise that follows helps you to be able to voice your 'NO' so that you can protect yourself and have a clear sense of a powerful boundary. It helps you to get your power back and to feel a strong connection with yourself.

Before you start this exercise, make yourself comfortable in a place where you won't be disturbed. Take a deep breath in and a long out-breath. Do this a few times. Become aware of your body and notice how resourced you are. Feel into your body for a sense of comfort. If you can't find one, then look around the room for something that is pleasing to you. If you are feeling tension in any part of your body, notice this and then bring your awareness to the feeling of comfort or another resource that you have found. If you are at all activated, take a little time to lower your activation levels by moving your attention backwards and forwards between your feeling of activation and the feeling of comfort or resource that you have established for yourself. Bring yourself into your 'window of tolerance'; the place within yourself where you are aware of any activation, but not overwhelmed by it.

STEP 1: Imagining

Now, without doing anything, IMAGINE yourself in the centre of your circle and saying the word

'NO'.

Notice any sensation in your body. This sensation could be tingling, a feeling of energy streaming, trembling, or any other subtle feeling that you didn't notice before. Wait a while for the sensation to clear and settle.

STEP 2: Speaking out Loud

Now say the word

'NO'

out loud. Don't say it in a pleading way, say it strongly - as if you really mean it. Notice how strongly you were able to say it. You can practice so that it gets stronger each time. Now check into your body and again notice any sensation. Notice what the sensation feels like and where it is in your body. Pause for a while and allow it to clear. Doing this exercise slowly is very important.

Again, say the word 'NO'. Feel what happens in your body and allow sensations to clear.

STEP 3: More imagining

This time I want you to imagine saying

'THAT IS MY LIMIT'.

Now notice what is happening in your body. Again, notice any kinds of subtle sensation. Give space for these sensations to clear. For instance, you may feel tingling or subtle trembling in a part of your body.

STEP 4: More speaking out loud

Repeat out loud as strongly as you can.

'THAT IS MY LIMIT'.

Again, notice what is happening in your body. If you feel sensation such as energy moving or streaming in your limbs, give this time to clear. If you don't feel anything, that is fine, but don't rush this exercise. The slower you go and the more attention that you pay to your body, the more powerful this exercise is.

STEP 5: Putting the words together

Say again strongly, the two parts combined now.

'NO, THAT IS MY LIMIT'.

Give your body a chance to process any energies that are moving in your body. Notice any other feeling coming up, either as sensation or emotion. You may have any kind of emotion arising such as sadness or anger. Notice how that feels in the body. Which part of your body is this emotion in? What are the physical sensations of this emotion? For instance, do you feel contracted or tense where the emotion is? Is there a feeling of hollowness or coldness or heat? Or any other physical sensation linked to the emotion?

Repeat this stage as many times as you need to until any sensations that have been coming up, finally begin to clear. You can do the exercise over several days if necessary. When all the sensations and emotions have processed through you can move onto the next stage. If you have an intense feeling of anger coming up, then slow the exercise down or stop it and go for a brisk walk or other physical activity. What is happening is that the physical energy that was frozen in your body is beginning to release.

It is very important that frozen trauma energies are released slowly so that you do not become overwhelmed.

This exercise is part of the following exercise below. You can do them together or in two separate parts. Listen to your body as to what feels right for you. If it feels too much for now, you can do the next part on a separate occasion.

Exercise 7

Physical Gesture of STOP

This exercise builds a greater strength of power and authority in your body and helps you to protect your boundaries.

Sitting up straight or standing up is best for this exercise. Before you start the exercise, feel your feet on the ground. Now take an in-breath and a long out-breath. Do this three times.

STEP 1: Imagining

Imagine raising your left arm with palm facing out in the stop gesture. Now notice what is happening in your body. As you did in the previous exercise, notice any feelings or sensations of trembling, shivering, tingling or any other subtle energy moving in your body. Give this time to clear from your body. Also, notice any emotion and the physical sensation that accompanies it. By now you know how to titrate and pendulate this feeling with a resourced feeling. Repeat the exercise in your imagination and include the word 'STOP' with the gesture. Check any somatic sensation and any emotion arising from this. Again, give it time to clear.

STEP 2: Preparing your muscles

The next stage is more than very subtle. You are not yet physically doing it. You are preparing your muscles to do the movement. Just think about which muscles you will have to contract in order to make the movement of raising your arm into the 'stop' gesture.

Whilst preparing your muscles, imagine saying STOP'. Notice what has happened in your body sensation and emotions. Let any discharge clear.

STEP 3: Physically making the movement

*It is important that you do this **SLOWLY**.*

It is time to physically make this movement. Raise your left arm **SLOWLY** with your palm turned out in a strong, clear way that signals 'STOP'. Say the word at the same time. Do it as if you really mean it with authority. Your intention is that you definitely are going to stop what is happening. Hold it for 30 seconds. Now release and feel what is happening in your body. What sensations are there? What emotions are arising? Where are you feeling them? What do they feel like physically? Give yourself time to titrate these feelings and if you have any activation, pendulate it with a resourced feeling that you can find. Track this sensation and allow it to clear. If you need to resource yourself, do that.

STEP 4: Combining the movement and the words

It is important to do this SLOWLY.

Now the final stage of this exercise is to repeat the stop gesture and this time you add the words. 'STOP! NOW!! THAT IS MY LIMIT'. Do it strongly but slowly. Hold it for 30 seconds and release. Notice any tingling, trembling, streaming of energy. Notice any emotion and what it feels like physically. Allow enough time for any energy moving in your body to clear. Be conscious of what is stirred up by this exercise or if you are activated. The activation could be either way. You may be experiencing hyper-arousal, going into 'fight-or-flight', or hypo-arousal, and going into parasympathetic shock. You could find yourself agitated, or you could find yourself freezing or spacing out. You could be experiencing the feeling of dissociation. Should this be the case, then take time to resource yourself. It is important that you monitor your activation and know that it is a memory from the past and that you are entirely SAFE now. The past is over and done with. Bring yourself back to your window of tolerance.

If very activated, stop doing the exercise for today. Take time out to go for a walk or do something totally different and resourcing for yourself.

STEP 5: Doing the exercise on the right side of your body

When you are ready you can now go through the process with your right arm. You may want to do this now or you may want to do it in a different session. Work through the exercise slowly and track in the same way as you did on the left side. Noticing sensation and allowing it to clear from your body.

Titration is important because it allows enough healing energy to build to clear the trauma.

When you repeat with your right arm, be sure that you go slowly and that you don't miss out any of the steps. The first step is to imagine the gesture. The second step is to prepare your muscles to make the gesture. The third step is to make the gesture. The fourth step is to make the gesture with the word STOP. The fifth step is to make the gesture with the word 'STOP! NO! THAT IS MY LIMIT'. In between each step, allow time to feel any sensation or emotion and give yourself space for that to clear. You may experience energy streaming through your limbs. You may feel tearful. Whatever is happening is okay. You are completely safe and the past event where you became traumatised is over and done with. It is important to continually remind yourself of this. Should you be in a situation in your present life where someone is stepping over your boundaries, then you will now be stronger to deal with this.

"Saying No - brought up so much fear - I felt like I was being cheeky, naughty, aggressive and again like I had no right to tell others what to do. I also became aware of a deep need to NOT be angry or aggressive. The strength of my rejection of aggression was so strong... I find the aggression of others so awful that I refused to display it myself." Dr Marion Bevington

(Marion is learning the power of saying No in her life.)

Completion and Celebration:

When you have completed this exercise, take time to go and celebrate. If you do just one arm and then come back on a different occasion to do the second one, then celebrate after the first one and again after the second one. Celebration of achievements is really important. It gives your body the signal that it is moving forward and that you are achieving success.

Take it slowly - it is more powerful that way.
Remember: 'Small gains build victories.'

Pushing Exercises.

This next series of exercises are designed to help you build a sense of power in your body and to release frozen trauma energies.

If you are traumatised, it indicates that at the point when the traumatic event happened, you felt overwhelmed and powerless to stop it.

You may have initially been activated into 'fight-or-flight' but it is likely that your nervous system was overwhelmed and, at some level, your body felt that it was about to die. You would have gone into parasympathetic shock at that point.

The reality is that this experience was all in your past. It may be that you are currently facing a difficult situation, but you can heal from this past traumatising event.

The first step is to know that the previous event is over and that you have survived it.

It is over and you have the potential to totally heal.

Human beings are remarkably powerful and have incredible abilities. Even if you are feeling powerless at the moment, you have the same possibility to heal as every other human. Even if you are not aware of it, you are creating a reality and an outcome in this very moment. By becoming more conscious of your ability to create, you can utilise it to your best advantage, rather than recycling the illusion that you are about to die.

It is now time for you to create the reality in which you are strong and capable of having the life that you want, and that you are 100% committed to that.

These pushing exercises help to release the frozen trauma energies that are stored in your limbs. In the past, at the time of the traumatising event(s), the emergency situation that you were in initiated a response in your body, an attempt to escape, fight back, protect yourself or protect someone else. You were not able to complete the movement because the circumstances became too overwhelming. That experience is over and now you can complete the movement.

Exercise 8

Pushing Arms

For this exercise, it is important to find something or someone that you can push against. As you push, it is important that you feel some resistance but that the person or object that you are pushing against, then is able to be pushed away.

The best thing is to do it with someone who can be sensitive, and with whom you feel safe. They need to be able to just push gently back against your hands but eventually let you push them. It is a delicate balance of how much resistance you experience as you push. It is important that you do not get triggered into the feeling of powerlessness, but instead, experience yourself as being able to powerfully push away. It is also important that you do not have anxiety about hurting the other person. You have to both feel confident that this is not going to happen. If at all anxious about this, you can arrange some cushions or soft furniture for them to fall on if necessary.

If you don't have a person to help you, you may want to do this in a therapy session with a practitioner skilled in trauma healing. Alternatively, you could find a piece of furniture to push against that will move, like a big chair on castors.

When you are ready, and you are feeling well resourced and comfortable, you can begin this exercise. Start by feeling your feet on the ground. Take an in-breath and then a long out-breath. Repeat this three times.

STEP 1: Imagining doing the exercise

Firstly, I want you to imagine doing the exercise. Imagine stretching out both your arms with your palms facing out and up in the pushing position. Then imagine pushing until the person or object is pushed out of the way. Now spend a moment and check into your body for sensations and emotions. Should you have images of some past traumatising event where you were being overwhelmed by someone and you could not push the person away, remind yourself that this is a memory. Check what is happening in your body. If you have any uncomfortable sensations, then find a way to resource yourself. Likewise, if you have a memory of an impending accident, an accident which you could not stop, then take time to resource yourself before going any further. Should these images or emotions be distressing, then give yourself time to resource fully before continuing with the exercise.

STEP 2: Preparing your muscles to push

When you are ready, you can do the next step; preparing your muscles to push. Notice which muscles you would have to use to push out. Lift your arms up into the pushing position and tense those muscles. Now relax the muscles. When you have done this, again check for any sensations and emotions. Notice what the emotions feel like physically in your body. If you have tingling, or streaming of energy, or trembling. Allow this to complete. If you need to resource, then do so. Make sure that you stay within your window of tolerance.

STEP 3: Actually pushing

Now you are at the actual pushing stage. Place your hands against the hands of the other person or the chair. Feel your feet firmly rooted in the earth and lean with your body into the push, ensuring that you maintain your sense of balance. Just push slowly and powerfully until the person or the chair gives way and moves. Now stop and feel into your body. What is happening for you in this moment? Take care to check carefully. Let any movement, streaming energy or other sensation complete its flow.

Repeat this exercise several times in the same way, each time checking the feeling in your body. Then, after several repeats, you can add in the words, said in a strong voice. **'STOP! NO! THIS IS MY LIMIT'**. When you have completed, check into the sensation in your body and any emotions that have come up for you. Give them time to complete and drain from your body; resource if you need to.

CELEBRATION:

Now it is time to celebrate the completion of this exercise. What will you do for yourself to mark the occasion? Can you go for a pleasant walk, treat yourself to a nice lunch, buy yourself a treat, or take a long comforting bath? Or perhaps something else that you really enjoy doing.

Pushing Arms - this process was fascinating as it needed me to really tune in to my body movements, strength, sensations and the feelings that arose as I connected to my own power and my own ability to create and protect my own space".   Dr Marion Bevington

---

Exercise 9

Pushing Legs

We also hold frozen trauma energies in our legs. Our legs are important to run to escape, to catch something or someone, or to kick out at something. We can also use them for climbing, which may be very useful in an emergency.

What was it that your legs were needing to do for you at the time that you were traumatised?

Legs were particularly important for you in the womb because they were the means by which you were able to initiate your birth. At birth, you felt the impulse to get born and then made the movement that triggered the onset of labour for your mother.

When you are ready, and you have completed the exercises with your arms, you can start with your legs. You will again need to find a helpful partner or a fairly solid piece of furniture to push against. Find yourself a comfortable spot where you can lie on the floor on your back. Make sure that you are feeling safe and that you will not be disturbed.

STEP 1: Imagining

Now imagine putting your legs up in the air with your calves at right angles to your thighs and your feet upright ready to push against something. You are just imagining pushing; not physically moving. When you have done that, notice how you are feeling in your body. What sensations or emotions are you feeling? Allow any sensation or energy to clear, and any emotion to settle.

STEP 2: Preparing to push

The next stage is again preparing your muscles to push. Get everything in place and then, just as you are about to push, stop and relax. Be aware of any sensation in your body that needs to clear. It might be energy streaming, or also some emotion may have been stimulated. If you have any difficult memories come up, then just allow them to settle again, telling yourself that the past is over with and that you are safe now.

STEP 3: Actually Pushing

This time you actually push. If you have a person helping you, get them to place their hands on your feet and give you some resistance. Alternatively, the person can also lie on their back on the floor and place their feet on your feet. When you push, they need to let their arms or feet move back whilst maintaining contact with your feet. You need to push slowly and surely, and gradually push them away until they can no longer maintain contact. If you have a piece of furniture, then place your feet on it where you have solid contact and begin to push, initiating the push from your body so that it is extending all the way through your legs. Be aware of sensations as you push. When the push is completed, and the person or the furniture is pushed away, notice any sensations such as trembling, or energy clearing in your legs. Be conscious of any arising emotion. Resource if you need to.

STEP 4: Repeat

Now repeat the process again. It is like pumping out the stuckness in your legs from when you weren't able to use them to save yourself. Imagine the stuck feeling emptying out of your legs; feel how powerful they are, especially your quadricep muscles which are in your thighs. These are the strongest muscles in your body. After you have pushed away, again notice any sensation. Is it the same as last time? Is it more or less sensation? Are there temperature changes in your body? Do you need to repeat this exercise a third time?

STEP 5: Combining Pushing with Words

If you are ready, you can now do the same pushing exercise combined with the words. **'STOP! NO! THIS IS MY LIMIT'**. Say it strongly and clearly, and push at the same time with a strong intention of not allowing anything over your boundary. When you have done this, check for sensation, energy levels, and emotions arising. Allow them to clear.

CELEBRATE, CELEBRATE, CELEBRATE!

Well done! Now you can go and celebrate. You deserve it. You have done a big piece of work. Before you do, take a few minutes to note how you felt doing the exercise; write it on your chart or put something in your progress diary.

Further work with the pushing exercises

To be able to release more of the frozen trauma energies, you can do the pushing exercises when you have a certain level of activation. For instance, if you find yourself experiencing anger, anxiety, or depression, then take the time to do the exercise and give yourself the opportunity to titrate the experience with some well-resourced breaks.

Exercise 10

Preparing to run or fight

You can also work on the feeling of needing to run or to fight. You go through the process described above of first imagining that you are doing this, either running or fighting. The second step is imagining preparing your muscles to run or fight. The final step is actually tensing your muscles ready to run or to fight. You hold them in tension for around 15 – 30 seconds and then release the tension. Repeat three times. At each release point, give time for any energy to drain from your body.

Releasing the energy of anger through your fists:

In this version of the exercise, you are go through the same process as previously. Firstly imagine doing the exercise. Secondly prepare the muscles to do the exercise. Thirdly do the physical movements. It is important to do it slowly and to give sufficient time for the energy to discharge through your limbs in waves of subtle tingling or trembling, or whatever it is that your body wants to do.

First, imagine clenching your right fist, and then your arm muscles and then your shoulder muscles and your jaw. Hold it, then slowly release it. Now notice what is happening in your body after this imaginary exercise. Give it space to release if it starts to do that.

Next, physically do the exercise, slowly curling your hand into a fist, clenching, tightening your arm muscles, your shoulders and then your jaw. As a variant on this or another step, you can slowly move your arm into an extended position as if hitting out at someone. Do it REALLY SLOWLY. Then gradually and slowly release. BREATH deeply and become aware of any subtle feelings in your body, such as trembling or any other kinds of sensations. Wait until it clears before repeating the exercise.

You can do this exercise several times on one side, and then switch to the other. Notice the difference between the two. Give full time for the discharge of any sensations.

Be guided by your experiences of arising sensations, images, memories, sounds, and emotions. If these experiences happen, then give them time to clear. If it becomes intense, then take time out, stop the exercise and resource yourself. You can come back to it at another time. Best to do it slowly as it is more effective that way.

Exercise 11

Mindfulness Meditation - Tracking the way that you embody emotions.

If you were able to go through the previous exercises without feeling too activated or disturbed, then you may be able to move on to this next stage.

Sit down in a comfortable space where you know that you are not going to be disturbed. Take an in-breath and a long out-breath. Repeat this three times.

Now notice how resourced you are. Do the resourcing work to feel comfortable and safe in your body. Now allow yourself to just let your awareness move through your body sensations. Start at the tip of your toes and gradually move up through each area of the body. Is there any particular, noticeable sensation in any part of the body that you are exploring? Notice if you have any tension or familiar sensations. Is there a particular pattern of sensation in your body that you recognise? Allow yourself to be curious about these areas. Choose one particular area that is attracting your attention? Settle your awareness into that area and ask 'what else is there here for me to explore or understand?'. Sit with the sensation and notice if it moves or changes; whether it diminishes or amplifies. How deep does it go into your body? What area does it extend to in your body? What is the temperature in that area? Does it gradually merge with the rest of your body at its edges or is there a sudden, sharp transition? Does it have a colour? Is the colour the same all the way across the area? Does this area connect, or relate in any way, to any other area in your body? Is there a texture or a sound, or does it conjure up a sense of something familiar? Is there an emotion associated with it? What is the emotion? Can you sit with that emotion or sensation? Hold it in your attention with a **wide perceptual awareness.** Do not focus on it intensely.

Remember that you can take time to resource yourself if you need to. If the exercise brings up some strong emotion or memory, then allow yourself to negotiate a relationship with it. The idea is that you can begin to form a connection with it without being overwhelmed and over-activated. How much can you stay 'present' and how much do you need to distance yourself from it? Negotiate this safe relationship so that you can witness it like watching a film. Do not get sucked into it.

What happens to the feeling, the emotion, and the sensation as you do this?

When you feel like you have explored this sufficiently, then bring your attention back to a sense of comfort in your body. Notice if your body feels different in any way.

Bring the meditation to a close and take time to write about it in your diary or make a note about the experience on your chart.

How was the exercise for you? If it brought up challenging feelings or memories, then you might want to wait for a few days before you repeat it. See what else is stimulated by it. Notice your dreams and activation states. Take time over the next couple of days to really ground and resource yourself. If all is well and you are not overly activated by painful memories, it would be beneficial to begin to do this as part of your daily routine.

Our bodies hold the full story to everything that has happened to us - they are also the pathway to recovery.

Each exercise that we have done here so far has been helping you to unravel and release patterns which were imprinted in your body from those occasions when you experienced traumatising events. Those events had an effect on your nervous system that we call trauma. Once we have trauma, our bodies are no longer the same. We have to work backwards and unravel what has happened, and restore our nervous systems to a calmly functional way of being. Again, our bodies are the pathway to doing this. This is because our primitive brains cannot be changed by our thinking brain. The way to change what the primitive brain is doing is through tracking sensation in our bodies and releasing frozen movements.

It may be that when you became traumatised, your body was trying to do something to protect you which subsequently became frozen in time. You may have been in the process of stopping yourself falling, or orientating yourself to a sudden danger. You could have been wanting to curl up to defend yourself, or perhaps you wanted to push someone or something away from you. All these movements, as well as body postures, can be frozen into the body, giving rise to symptoms such as extreme tension, joint pain, nervous tics, and feelings of anger or anxiety. As we explore these 'holding patterns' in the body, we have the possibility of completing the actions that got frozen. As we complete them, they then disappear and our bodies change. Once gone, these frozen actions are no longer triggering our nervous system and we can settle more fully into the present moment.

You might want to go a little deeper in the following sessions and let your body show you the places where it got frozen, You might also explore more subtle states of stuck energy patterns. Those that are less obviously physical. To do this you have to be in the mode of 'allowing' and not having any expectations of the outcome. You must be in a state of 'enquiry'. Your body has many stored memories and experiences that want to be expressed somatically. Your body is very ready to heal, you just need to get out of the way of this process. You do this by creating a supportive environment which focusses on being curious and compassionate.

You could call this a space of compassionate self-enquiry.

In the following exercises, you will discover this is not just a physical experience but also an energetic one. There are generative healing forces at work which, as you listen in a very still and sensitive way, you will begin to experience. Generative forces are forces within the body that are creative and, in this instance, help to release restrictions to bring about healing.

Each person's perceptual awareness style is very different. Everyone experiences themselves in a different way. In the following exercises, you can discover how you personally experience these forces at work within your own body. When I am quiet and still enough, and turning my attention inwards, I experience subtle spirals of energy which are pulsating. They increase a feeling of expansion and spaciousness in my body through initiating a series of subtle physical movements. As a Craniosacral Practitioner, I have witnessed many people going through these processes of release. They have each had different ways of 'being'. There is no right or wrong way. This is about 'allowing' yourself to unfold in all your own uniqueness.

Setting up a regular time and space to do this work is very helpful. You begin to train your body.

Exercise 12

Mindfulness Meditation – Allowing your body to express movement

Prepare yourself and your space now so that you can explore some more healing with yourself. Make sure that you will not be disturbed and that you are warm and comfortable. Remind yourself that in this moment you are completely safe and that anything that you experience is body memory.

Either lie down or sit in a comfortable, supported position. Take a deep in-breath and a long out-breath. Repeat this another couple of times. Be aware of the contact that your body is making with the place that you are lying or sitting. Settle your attention into your body. Notice where you have a sense of comfort and resource in your body. Focus your attention into that resourced comfortable sensation. Allow the sensation to grow and spread if it wants to. Breath into it.

When this comfortable resourcing sensation is fully established, allow your attention to move to any other sensation in your body. There will often be a place or a sensation that will 'call' your attention. Settle your awareness into that new sensation. **Notice what qualities it has.** How would you describe it? Does it have a shape or a colour? How big is it? Where is it in your body? Does it move? Is there a texture or a density? How else can you describe it?

Explore its edges and how it changes where it connects with other parts of your body. Does it have the same qualities across the whole of the area? If not, then how does it change? What is different in one part of it or another part? Does it change in intensity?

Now the important thing is to **hold a wide perceptual awareness**. Do not focus intensely into that sensation. You are holding the sensation in your awareness but also being aware of other sensations in your body. You are not attaching to any particular one. Now ask yourself, where is the 'fulcrum' for this sensation and experience? Where is the origination point? Is it in or outside of your body? If outside of your body, where is it? Allow yourself to feel more subtle sensations or energy movements. You may see or hear them or simply have a sense of 'something'. Your experience may be very different from mine. I am simply giving you a road map for you to explore your own experience.

You will begin to find your own way of knowing these things.

When you have found a fulcrum, then sit with that in your awareness. If something difficult or painful comes up, negotiate a safe distance from it. How can you be present with it and not be overwhelmed by it? For example, you can imagine that you are watching something on a video, so that you are creating some distance and are not completely merged with the experience. Practice going both closer and further away from the experience. Notice your activation levels; are you about to be overwhelmed or is the experience manageable for you? Evaluate how resourced you are. You need to have a foundation of being well resourced. You are powerful and you can explore this without being overwhelmed. Being well resourced will help you enormously.

You may be aware of subtle energies at work. What is happening in bringing your attention to this fulcrum, is that the healing energies, or generative forces, are at the point of 'decoupling' from the forces of resistance and stagnation. It is imperative that you simply witness and do not put any active engagement of any kind, mental, emotional, spiritual, or physical into this experience. This is why it is important to hold a wide perceptual awareness. By creating this spaciousness in your attention, you are not interfering with the process. It is simply unfolding. Even focussed attention is an interference in the process. You need to have a soft engagement with it. Being aware of it but in an entirely unfocussed way. If you really intensify your attention into any area, it will intensify the uncomfortable feelings that are there. Likewise, if you start having judgments about what you are experiencing, this also disrupts the healing that is happening here. Be as open and spacious as you can be.

Compassionate Enquiry is about witnessing yourself and holding consciousness around your experience; Be 'present' to yourself and don't try to change what you are observing. Notice the continual stream of consciousness.

As you sit with this experience, you may also begin to have a sense that your body would like to make a movement. It may be very, very subtle. **Pay attention to it and allow it.** Let it unfold really slowly. The slower and the more attention that you pay to it, the more subtle levels of stagnated, stuck energy and pain will be able to release from your body. Let the movement unfold little by little so that you are titrating the experience. You may be aware of subtle energy pulsating and even spiraling. You may begin to feel warmth and relaxation or expansion in the area. Don't be attached to any outcome. Don't try to make anything happen. It is always different and your experience is unique. Emotions may come up or even just tears spring to your eyes. Just allow. There is nothing more to do except to be open to the experience.

Sometimes you may feel that you need to make a sound. Allow this to happen as well. Just explore and let whatever needs to unfold, happen. You may make nonsensical sounds or animal sounds, or you may have words that come to you. It may be a shout or a loud cry or even a scream. It is all fine and part of the healing process.

Even though you are tracking these experiences in a quiet, focussed way, you may sometimes experience big jolts or jumps happen to your body. They are discharges from your sympathetic nervous system. It is fine for them to happen. They are releasing stuck energy. It could also be lots of little jolts. Or it could be that your limb makes a sudden movement. The movement may be accompanied by a sound, a call, or a shout. After this happens you may find yourself much more deeply relaxed. Whatever happens, it is all part of the experience, Stay curious and continue to witness. You are entirely safe, and your body is expressing and releasing memories.

If you feel overly activated at any point, then you can return to your resourcing. Find a point of comfort in your body and settle your attention back in this until it is well established again. You can also come out of the session at any point that you like. You won't lose anything by stopping the session. Your body is on a healing journey and it will always pick it up again next time you create the space for it to happen.

Pacing your session:

You will have a sense that there is a particular experience unfolding which will normally come to a natural end. Your consciousness will tend to come to a completion point with what you are witnessing. There will be a completion point where you are back in your normal reality.

Be aware that sometimes, these kind of experiences can follow one after another in a continuous way. Do not continue for a long time if these experiences seem to want to go on and on. Sometimes, when there is a lot of content or a high nervous system charge, there is a tendency to 'keep going for it'. You need to be aware of your body's energy resources and pace yourself so that you do not become tired. This may be more of a problem if you have a history of fatigue. Healing takes a lot of energy; it is important to rest, to sleep, and to nourish yourself at a high level to provide the necessary energy for the process.

My personal experience of doing this practice:

When I do this work – it can be dramatically different from session to session. Start with sitting and then notice if there is something 'coming up for you'. The more I can be in a place without time pressure, fear of intrusion by telephone calls or someone liable to need my attention, the deeper I can go.

There are certain familiar somatic patterns that come up for me and they may have a different 'flavour' each time I witness them. Over many years there has been a gradual releasing and unfolding of my personal story. I used to have many large energy jolts and sudden dramatic movements of my head to the left, which I believe was associated with my being stuck in the birth canal. It relates to a pattern of tension down my left side, and other left-sided symptoms that I have. Sometimes, when I am just being still and dropping more deeply into an expansive place, a scream comes out of nowhere. After this happens there is sometimes a big feeling of warmth and expansiveness in my shoulders or chest.

Sometimes, I have gone into deep emotional experiences. Wells of sadness can open up and engulf me, but I always keep an awareness of myself experiencing this sadness. I am not overwhelmed by it. This is important. It is about witnessing, not identifying with and merging into the experience. After this has happened, I have experienced profound healing around my heart area. Memories may come up from times in the womb. I may have a story running in my head at the same time. I just witness this as well without trying to interfere with it, attach to it, or believe it. Whether it is true or not does not matter. Sometimes the story is about a past life scenario where parts of my body were hurt or wounded, or where I died. Again, I don't attach to this, only witness it. It may or may not be an accurate memory. It is important not to put labels on these experiences. In reality, we cannot know what the source of the   is or about. What is important to me, is it is an expression of my psyche which needs to express itself in a particular format for me to be able to understand how I am embodying an experience.

Exercise 13

Releasing higher levels of Activation.

Your own experiences will be quite unique, and you will be healing on all levels as you give yourself space. Should you come up with lots of activating memories, you can release the frozen trauma energies by going back to the Exercises 6 through to 10 according to which is appropriate to your present experience. These are the pushing exercises.

When you first did those exercises, I advised to start them at a low level of activation. You can now commence them with a certain level of activation. If, for instance, in your meditation, you experience a lot of tension within a part of your body that holds an accompanying memory of being forced into a situation, you can take that level of activation as your starting point, and, pushing it away with your hands and feet, say 'STOP! NO! THIS IS MY LIMIT'. Work through this with both your hands and feet. Please be aware to stay mindful so that you do not get pulled into overwhelm. Stay in the witness awareness as you are doing this.

CELEBRATION TIME:

Well done for getting this far. Now is the time to celebrate.

When we celebrate, it brings completion to something that we have been working on. This is a good starting point for moving forward: it gives a sense of achievement and progression. Often when we are healing, it can feel like we are stuck in the same feelings forever. Even though it is changing, we don't necessarily see it; celebrating highlights the shifts that are happening. If you have got through these exercises so far, then take time out to do something that is fun and enjoyable for yourself.

KEEPING TRACK OF YOUR PROGRESS

Make sure that you are keeping track in your diary and activation chart. You need to get a feel for how your nervous system is changing, and how your window of tolerance is getting wider. Read back and see what has happened so far, and what might have changed. Get a sense of what you need to do more of. Also keep a track of your dreams, and the daily victories that are happening for you.

Should you feel that you are still overwhelmed and lost with this process, it may be that you also need someone to help you. You may want to have some trauma resolution sessions with an experienced trauma therapist. You can search on the internet for people to help you. Look for therapists skilled in appropriate body-orientated type of trauma therapy. It could be Somatic Experiencing, Body Centred Psychotherapy, Family Systems Therapy, or maybe EMDR.

Exercise 14

Practicing Dual Awareness

What do you do when you can't connect into your body sensations?

If you have experienced severe body injury or physical abuse—sexual or otherwise—you may find it very challenging to connect into a body awareness. You may find that you cannot sense anything; your body might feel numb, empty, or simply 'not there'. Parts of your body may feel hollow, or you may feel simply 'bored' by the process. All such feelings could indicate that you have quite a high degree of shock in your system. You may also find yourself 'spacing out' when you attempt to focus on your body, or anything else that is remotely challenging in your life. If this is happening to you, then practicing dual awareness will help you through this stage.

Dual awareness is important when your autonomic nervous system is activating you into a feeling of impending danger, yet you are not in a remotely dangerous situation. If you go with the signals, you can feel highly anxious and stressed, or numbed out and shut down.

It could be that you begin to find yourself in a highly charged and agitated emotional state; or maybe you have thoughts wildly circulating in your mind, repeating the same ideas over and over. Maybe you are even getting flashbacks of a situation that happened. They may be true-to-life pictures in front of your eyes, or sounds that are convincing. These kinds of hallucinations are a result of the trauma; they will go away as you heal yourself. If this is the case, the activation has been so intense that your perceptions are being distorted and altered by your state.

The way to heal this state is to develop enough self-awareness and self-reflection to allow you to see beyond the danger signals and flashbacks from your primitive brain.

Here are some steps that you can follow to help you with this process:

STEP 1: Awareness of Activation

Do you remember your window of tolerance?
Whereabouts, within it, are you?

It is important at this time to be aware of your level of activation, or, at the minimum, to be aware that you are activated. It may be a high level of anxiety as expressed through tension in the body, shallow breathing, and agitation. Or you may feel dissociated, disconnected, and 'bored'—as expressed by brain fog, limp limbs, weakness, jelly legs, or other similar symptoms. Ask yourself, *'how activated am I right now?' 'What can I do to change this, and to calm myself down again?'*

When you notice that this high level of activation is coming on, can you turn your awareness to your senses so that they can check out the reality in the present moment?

You might, first of all, reach out to pick up a soothing sensory object such as a smooth stone, cuddly toy, or soft blanket. Or play some soothing music. Focus on these pleasant sensations.

STEP 2: Awareness of information coming in through your senses.

What information are your senses giving you? Perhaps to make it easier, you can have a helpful check list to hand.

Consider all your senses, including your sense of balance and where you are in space. What can you see, hear, smell, touch, and where is your body in the space that you are occupying? If you are getting auditory or visual flashbacks, what clue can you get that this is not a real experience? Where within yourself can you identify that this is the past, not the present moment? As you follow the actions suggested below, the flashbacks may stop, and you can recognise that they were not real.

STEP 3: Taking action and exploring with your senses.

Your primitive brain is telling you that you are in danger. Is this real? Can you see or hear anything dangerous? When you check things out with your conscious awareness, do you perceive a threat of any kind? It is even worth going a little bit further and doing things like getting up and walking around the room and looking carefully at everything to check if there is danger. You can look under furniture and behind curtains, or any other place that you feel that danger might be lurking. Be silly even. Pick up a book, or a cushion even, or turn over a stone. It is not about what is logical; it is about getting back into your primitive orientating response. You are calming your primitive brain.

As you do this exploratory activity, notice—if you are able—what begins to happen in your body. Walk around the space you are in and see if you can access the power in your legs. If you are in a room, go and open the door and step outside. What does this feel like? What changes in your body as you do this? Even if you can't feel much in your body, notice if you now begin to feel 'more here'. Maybe you feel more grounded, or you begin to breath more deeply. Perhaps your vision begins to clear a little.

STEP 4: Reassure yourself and update reality.

Take time to tell yourself: *'Although it felt like I was in danger and I was getting activated, the reality is, that right here, right now—in this moment—I am well and safe.'*

Take time—after you have done this exercise and calmed down—to make a note of the experience. Note how activated you were, and what changed. Write in your journal, or enter something on your activation chart.

This process is doing two things. Firstly, it is bringing you into the 'present moment' by updating your nervous system and letting it know that you are, in fact, quite safe now. It is also completing the 'orientating' process that you were not able to do at the time of the traumatic event. This, in itself, will release frozen trauma energies and be a healing process for you. By documenting your experience, you are building more self-awareness, which means in future you are less likely to get so activated.

STEP 5: A daily practice.

It is good to practice this on a daily basis, even if you are not having difficulty accessing your somatic awareness; it will help to build your sense of safety, and gradually lower the intense anxiety and fear that may be dominating your life.

STEP 6: Post reminders to yourself.

If the above exercise of telling yourself that you are safe in the present moment is challenging and you are still caught up in your activation, then write some notices and pin them up in key places. Write things like 'the anxiety is caused by memories', 'there is nothing here that can harm me', 'I am safe'. You might also remind yourself to breath. Six, really good, deep breaths with very long out breaths helps lower the amount of adrenaline being pumped into your system, and is very calming. Also, a brisk walk will use up the adrenaline. Should you tend to wake in the night with a high level of activation, you can have reassuring notes up where you can easily see them. Soothing sensory objects can also help you, as can calming music.

CHAPTER 5

Working with your emotions

Trauma is a physical problem in your body. It is a result of what is happening in your nervous system. You may have circling thoughts and intense emotional states that accompany it. To heal trauma, it is important to do the work that we have been describing previously, before trying to address your emotional states.

Once you have a sense that the immediate intensity of the reactivity is beginning to settle, and you have started to access emotional content in your meditations — or if you know that there are some pressing emotional issues — you can employ various processes to help release and transform them.

When you have been shattered, distressed, and traumatised, there are likely to be a lot of simmering emotions that need to be released and integrated. Here we explore *some* of the major emotional states that are commonly experienced in trauma. You may have other complex emotions, not listed here, that are causing you pain. However, if you learn how to work with the emotions covered here, it will give you the means to explore and heal the other ones.

Anger

Anger is a natural life force energy that rises up to protect us when we are in a life-and-death situation. It is biologically designed to make us as powerful and strong as possible. When we are thus triggered by our nervous system, from our primitive brain, we can do physical and wildly aggressive actions way beyond our normal capability.

In addition to this, our frontal cortex — where we have the capacity for rational thought, conscience, and self-reflection — is switched off. This is why it is not possible to reason or talk to someone who is in a rage. This capacity of anger is meant to be used infrequently, but problems arise when we become traumatised. It is common to become constantly triggered into big outbursts of anger, and to feel a constant underlying irritation that is difficult, unpleasant, and even unsafe for others to be around. Is this something that happens to you? If so, are you aware of the effects on others, and the impact on your relationships? Does this bring a layer of shame as well, because you feel that you do not have the capacity to control this? Do you, in turn, seek some justifiable defense that you can hide behind? Do you form a belief system that makes it okay to be angry? Perhaps you think that certain people, organisations, ethnic groups, or bank managers 'deserve it'? Perhaps you believe it is right and purposeful to be angry with your children, because they need discipline or need to show you respect?

When you understand the immense physical power that anger can give you, you might question the wisdom of acting it out randomly.

Trauma gets passed down the generations. When locked into our own trauma and the immense volatility of anger which is the fight reaction, we often unconsciously act this out on innocent people.

How many of us have already been deeply harmed through violence — either in a brutalised childhood, a violent relationship, or in a school, prison, or other institution run by people who are prone to anger due to their own trauma?

Just as with the other symptoms of trauma, it is possible to heal it. In doing so, you will feel better about yourself. Your life will flow more easily, and your relationships will be happier. Most importantly, you will NOT be passing trauma forward into the next, and subsequent, generations.

So how do you heal anger? There has been a great belief with past therapeutic approaches that we have to get our anger 'out' and then it is dealt with. This is a bit of a misconception. We are not a container filled with anger. We get angry as a result of a trigger that reminds us of a time when we were truly in a life-and-death situation. At those moments, our primitive brain will take us into fight-or-flight, and we will be angry. The more that we then thump, shout, scream, and threaten, the angrier we will get. This means that we are continually pumping adrenaline through our body, fueling the anger. Thus, in the process of getting it 'out' we are actually activating more and more anger. We finally stop when we are exhausted. However, this has not healed the anger; the trigger will still be there and, on another occasion, we can get angry again with the same or a similar trigger. So, the approach of thumping pillows and 'getting into our anger to release it' gives the appearance that something is happening that is very obvious, but it is not truly healing.

To heal anger, we need to heal the trigger. We need to be mindful about the anger, what is causing it and what we are doing with it when it comes. We have to update the primitive brain into normal, calm functioning so that the amygdala is not firing off inappropriately. We have to quieten and integrate other parts of the brain to work together in the present moment in a connected and conscious way. In this way, the primitive part of the brain can make the right choices. Again, it comes down to creating safety and well-being for the body, and for yourself.

Let us briefly look at triggers. Do you have a sense of what sets you off into feeling angry? It is useful to look at possible triggers that can upset people. They can be divided into three categories.

1. Thwarted Intentions
2. Unfulfilled Expectations
3. Undelivered Communications

1. Thwarted intentions

Do you tend to feel blocked in your life? Perhaps in the past, you had an intention that didn't work out. You had a vision that you couldn't fulfill, or a need that was never met that you had the intention to do something about. Or something that was going to happen, but something came in the way of it that resulted in you suffering? You never got the job, the education, or the person you loved, even though you had intended it to happen and you had worked towards it?

If you can relate to any of those ideas, take the time to write it down. Notice if there was more than one occasion when this happened. Is it still happening? Are you always on the lookout for this happening? Does it repeat itself in your life? Do you now have a belief system built around it? For instance, thoughts like — *"no matter how much I try, I never get what I want!"*

2. Unfulfilled expectations

This category is similar to the one above in that it can have a feeling of being let down, but it is subtly different. It is about anticipating that life is going to flow a certain way but something happens and it just doesn't go like that. There may have been the person that you always thought that you would marry who is killed, for instance. Or that you would have a large family but you find that you never meet a partner or can't have children. Or that your loved one will be with you forever, but leaves you for another person.

Did you have an expectation of a certain experience that you were sure would happen, that simply didn't happen for you. This wasn't about you having a thwarted intention, but rather that we can have expectations about life. We can have a sense of entitlement that can be quite legitimate. *"My father/mother was never there for me". "I was neglected or abused". "I didn't get the education or the job that I should have got". "My partner was not faithful to me".* This is about being-cheated in some way — life has robbed you; or a person, or organisation has robbed you. Or maybe God robbed you when your life was impacted by an accident where you lost use of limbs or senses.

Anger is usually a result of hurt or fear. Were you exposed to a lot of hurt? Do you have an inner narrative about injustice? It shouldn't have happened, or have been happening to me. I need to protest or attack to set the record straight.

It is easy to get stuck in anger and negative feelings about this, and it feels very justified. However, to be endlessly stuck in the feelings means that your life is even more stuck than the originally limiting event.

Sometimes our expectations of a situation — especially involving either our self or another person — can be unrealistic. We may be so caught up in our angry reaction that we do not realise that we want something that is just not possible from that person, that organisation, or our self.

For instance, you could be telling your partner, "if you loved me, you would..." (do something which is beyond the capability of that person. Fill in the gap!) Or you could be setting yourself a totally unobtainable target that then causes you to feel anger towards yourself because you can't do the impossible.

If something like that is happening for you, then take time to reflect on whether the thing that you are wanting to happen is reasonable and doable. Are you having feelings of frustration because you are trying to force this undoable situation? Can you simply accept that there are some things that you want to happen that simply are not going to, because either you, the person, or the situation, is simply not capable of producing that result. For instance, were you a child whose parents were endlessly fighting, and all you wanted was for them to be happy together? Did you get stuck longing for this, then angry because it was never going to unfold in the way that you wanted. Can you be with the feelings of frustration around this, knowing that there is nothing that you can do to change it?

Anger and Blame:

Do you find yourself blaming the other person for the impossible not being able to happen? Do you tend to feel that the suffering you are going through, is because of someone else or something else? Do you project your negative feelings and anger on to someone else, making them wrong for all the 'bad things happening'? Can you witness yourself fanning the flames of your own anger, making it worse and hating people more? Or do you fan it inwardly, hating and blaming yourself for circumstances you could not have changed? Very often there are situations that are simply beyond our control, and we have to surrender to that knowledge.

Anger hiding other feelings:

Anger can often be the externalisation of other deeper feelings that have not had a chance for expression. Anger is almost always a result of deep hurt or fear, and if we give ourselves the space to feel into that anger, we may find that there is a great amount of grief and sorrow, (they are differing degrees of a similar emotion) underneath.

It often happens that this grief and sorrow are just too painful to be with; it is easier to get angry rather than sit with intense emotional pain. Anger can also arise due to deep physical pain. It is hard to endure either emotional or physical pain over long periods of time. We may find ourselves erupting into anger because of intolerable pain from which there's little to no relief. Anger can also happen when we are highly stressed. When enduring long periods of stress, something has to 'give' at some point!

Anger can also be linked to deep shame. Shame is such an annihilating feeling to experience that often people will do anything to avoid it; they can flare up into anger at the slightest hint of having the shame exposed. The anger becomes a defensive shield, protecting you from feeling an unbearable feeling. If you find yourself suddenly becoming very aggressive when a 'raw nerve' is touched, take time to gain some awareness of what is really going on under the surface. Those are the feelings that can be healed. If we use anger to escape them, it will keep going, time after time. We can't empty out our anger, but we can take time to explore and transform the feelings that give rise to it. Then those feelings will no longer trigger the primitive brain nervous system reaction that takes us into fight-or-flight.

Another cause of anger is the dependant use of alcohol and drugs. Addiction of any kind is usually an indication of trauma; if you find that you are flaring up into anger when you have been using any of these intoxicating substances, then there is undoubtedly deep hurt and pain underneath that needs healing. It is always possible to heal, so give yourself the opportunity to do this.

Do you feel any resonance in the ideas here? Do you have feelings or thoughts coming up that are some version of this? Take time to write them down. Are there numerous instances? Can you find a similar thread that links these experiences together? Write about the connections.

3. Undelivered communications:

This can be another common cause of anger and frustration. Is there something that you haven't admitted to yourself. Or maybe something that you haven't said to someone else? Perhaps there are words that you have been longing to hear — such as an apology or a declaration of love? Or maybe something has been brewing and irritating you for a long time that you don't have the courage to face up to? Does it make you fly off the handle at yourself or the other person? Do you have a belief that if you say it, irrevocable damage will be done to that relationship, or in that situation? Is this an accurate assessment, or is it a fear-based judgement? Where does this belief come from? Have there been situations in the past like this?

Again, take time to write about this. At least get the undelivered communications written down on paper, together with the thoughts of what might happen if you were to say it. Perhaps you have a sense that someone is not saying something to you that they want to, and that makes you feel fearful and angry.

You may be expecting a rejection, or to be fired, and you are aware of the energy behind the unspoken words, pushing you away. Or maybe you know that someone really likes you but doesn't reach out and share their true feelings. Again, write it down and see what comes up.

Growing up in an angry household.

Another reason why people become angry is if they have grown up in household where anger is the style of interaction within the relationships. Did this happen to you? Did you learn anger as a way of living life? Did everyone talk to each other in an angry way, and is this your means of communication now? Do you use sarcasm, or aggressive expressions, as a means of endearment? Do you think it is weak to show someone that you love them, or that you care? Do you hide behind being 'tough' or 'hard'? Is this how you have had to get through life in order to stay safe?

Perhaps you grew up in a family where members were suffering addiction or alcoholism, or there was a very high level of stress? Maybe in a war zone or as a refugee. It could be that family members were lost, or there was trauma further back in the family line that was not mentioned and not resolved. All these experiences can lead to an uncomfortable atmosphere, and maybe unspoken words or unfulfilled expectations. Perhaps you have had to carry an unbearable burden for your family; maybe you were never shown love or tenderness, only violent anger or sullen cold withdrawal of feelings and disconnection. This is going to have an impact on the way that your nervous system behaves. It will affect the way that you can deal with, or tolerate, stress and frustration. It will distort your capacity to understand what is a reasonable expectation of yourself and others, and what is a distortion of what is humanely possible. It may mean that you do not have the social skills for love and tenderness, but only feel able to express through angry words and defensive behaviour. Or, maybe you have adopted 'humour'— with a subtle edge of aggression — as a defense?

All these ways of relating can leave you feeling very isolated, alone, and disconnected, which means that you may seek substances and activities that become addictive patterns to cover up the pain and emptiness of being alone.

If this is your kind of family, can you take time to think about this and write down what comes to you? What are the situations that come up mostly that cause you to interact in this way? Can you be aware of the times when you use language that could be considered as abusive but you haven't meant it that way? If you have grown up in an angry and abusive family, just take time to see how this is affecting your life and relationships now.

How to heal your anger:

Anger is such a volatile feeling that it can be challenging to heal. It can happen so quickly from the moment of getting triggered to the point when you might be in a full-blown rage. If you are using alcohol, which decreases social inhibitions, this can happen even more quickly. Anger can be frightening for other people to witness, and it can easily drive people away — especially if you tend to project your anger and blame people. It is hard for people to stay in a loving connection with you if you are attacking them and making them wrong.

Angry people tend to act out their anger very quickly. They may instantly be verbally or physically aggressive to someone they are with. Or if the person is not there, they may write or dictate an aggressive message to them as an attack.

If they don't feel that it is ok to send that anger out, they can 'act the anger in' turning against themselves in some self harming way. Either way they may do something in anger that they regret for the rest of their life.

The Dalai Lama says that anger is the most regrettable of all emotions, and we should do our best to not succumb to it.

It is often the case that people who act with anger are not really able to feel the anger, or tolerate the feeling of it. The activation into anger comes up very rapidly and is swiftly acted out. Or it can be acted inwards, into self-destructive behaviours, or risk-taking, or suicide. I have experienced a few times in my life when inwardly directed anger broke a part of my life for ever. There are some things that I deeply regret but can't change now. I have just had to come to terms with what I did, and have compassion for the self that was me at that time. I was hurting so badly but didn't know how to help myself.

> "There needs to be understanding that anger never helps to solve a problem. It destroys our peace of mind and blinds our ability to think clearly. Anger and attachment are emotions that distort our view of reality." The Dalai Lama

If this speaks to you and you can relate to it, are you able to start some self-enquiry here? Do you have the habit of engaging in undermining and self-defeating activities, and addictive patterns? What happens to you? Do you act out or act in? Or is it a combination of both? Or are you ashamed of your anger and try to hide it, or sit on it until it consumes you into depression and collapse? Can you own up to this, and have compassion for yourself? We all suffer in this way. By taking away the self-judgement, it gives an opportunity for the pain to dissolve.

To heal this anger, it is important to start feeling it.

Once you have identified the triggers that can cause you to be angry, you can work on how to feel your anger.

Being able to slow down the anger reaction:

The first step in healing your tendency to fly into anger, is learning to slow down the reaction. It will take a lot of self-awareness. As you are doing this, you are developing an inner muscle that will prevent you simply 'flying off the handle' and going into attack mode.

You need to identify the kind of situation that triggers your anger. Answer some of the questions above, develop some enquiry into the why's and wherefores of your anger. As you are building this self-awareness, start to notice when you get angry. How long do you remain angry? What helps you recover your equilibrium?

When you find yourself getting angry, try to take yourself out of the situation to somewhere that you can be quiet and self-reflective. Go somewhere away from the stimulus that is causing the reaction. If you tend to get angry when you drink, begin to track when your level of intoxication is taking you towards anger. Make choices that will stop you putting yourself into those vulnerable situations. This may not be easy, but ultimately, if you don't do it, no-one else can do it if or you.

If you are able to be somewhere quiet when you begin to get angry, notice what is happening in your body. Do you feel your jaw getting tight? Can you feel tension in your arms and shoulders? Or in your neck? What do you notice happening with your hands? Are they clenching into fists? Are your legs tense? Take time to track these sensations and to work to release them. Search for a place in your body where you don't feel tense. See if there is somewhere that you can feel comfortable. Move your awareness between these places and see what changes with the tension patterns.

You will discover that your muscles are beginning to tension in preparation. Your primitive brain is sending out signals that you are in danger. You have to run or to fight your way out of this situation. You need to learn how to turn off this preparation by giving your primitive brain a different set of information. When you can focus on good feelings in the body, then this activation will go down.

You may need to engage in some physical activity. Go for a long walk, or dance, or play a sport such as badminton; some form of exercise or energetic movement like running, or playing a sport, that will use up the energy that is now stored in your muscles through the adrenaline surge.

Another thing that you can do is the exercise of clenching your fist very slowly, holding it, then releasing it again. You can also do the pushing exercises discussed in Chapter 4, Exercises 6 through to 10.

These exercises are designed to release the frozen trauma energies and the activation of anger in your body.

See how long you can be with the feeling of anger in your body, being aware of it, and working slowly to discharge it. Choose to do this rather than acting the anger out into behaviour that will harm others and cause you regret.

You will need to journal with this and begin to unwind the thought patterns and self-justifying belief systems that are underpinning your anger. In the process of doing this you will need to build tolerance and compassion for yourself. Ultimately, you will understand that redirecting anger into more positive activities is the path to greater peace and freedom

---

"If you harm someone out of anger, you may feel some superficial satisfaction, but deep down you know it was wrong. Your confidence will be undermined. However, if you have an altruistic attitude, you'll feel comfortable and confident in the presence of others." The Dalai Lama

---

Shame

Do you feel overwhelmed by shame? Do you feel like it is all your fault and you deserve nothing, least of all love and respect?

Shame is a very common symptom of trauma. It can be expressed as a self-critical voice in your head, continually repeating how bad you are and what you have done wrong. It serves to make you small and want to hide. It can disconnect you from other human beings because you feel unworthy.

All humans need to find safety in connection; when they are eaten up with shame, it is very hard to connect. The feeling literally causes someone to shrink down and hang their head in shame. In this way, they are less visible.

How can you break the cycle of shame?

One way is to externalise the internal voice of shame. By writing the shameful thoughts down, you are getting them out of your head.

EXERCISE 15

Make a shame pack

Get a small stack of postcards and write your shameful thought on one of them, then turn the card over and write down the opposite, neutralising, thought.

For instance, the shameful thought might be *"I eat way too much, and I am hideous and grossly fat and unhealthy"*. Write that down, then ask yourself, *"if I was addressing someone else, would I speak to them in this way? Why would I speak to myself in such an abusive way?"* If you are a parent, you might consider if you would talk to your child like this, or whether you would hold them accountable for negative behaviour in a way that was loving.

Now turn the card over and write something like, "I could lose a few pounds but overall, I am taking the steps to have a healthier diet and life style, so the extra weight will soon shed"

Continue for each of your self-shaming thoughts, so that you are able to externalise them rather than running them in your mind. Gradually build a way whereby you can quickly neutralise the shameful thought and find a more creative, kind way to address issues that are causing you a problem.

STEP 2: Sharing with someone else

Find someone with whom you can connect and feel safe enough to share your shameful thoughts. If there is no-one then perhaps some therapeutic help would be appropriate. Take your shame pack with you. Share how you feel when you consider your abusive self-talk. Include ideas about how you could reach out to yourself in a more constructive, caring way, and what a difference this would make.

You could also write about this in your diary. Challenge yourself as to the validity of your shameful self-judgements. Put them into a perspective of what is really happening in your life.

Where did your shame come from?

Were you shamed as a child in order to control your behaviour?

It has been a common parenting practice to shame a child to make them stop a particular behaviour. Did your parents or carers have that parenting style? What was it that they said to you? Take time to think about this and write it down. Are the phrases that you are writing down similar to your internal shame statements?

When your parents shamed you, did it actually make you stop the behaviour? Did it encourage you to want to be 'good' for them? Or did it isolate you and cut off your connection to them? Is this now-internalised shame talk having the same affect with you in your connection with yourself? Does it also make you stay out of connection with other people? If this is the case then you might want to again identify where your shame thoughts came from originally, and build some compassion for the 'little you' who was shamed in order to be controlled.

This kind of parenting style can be very damaging for children. When parents shame their children, it causes the children to feel like their parents are not truly seeing them. They are calling them bad because some core need in the child may be lacking, and the child's behaviour is reflecting the pain of what he or she is going through. It is now doubly wounding to be made to be ashamed because their very own needs are not met. It can leave a child feeling like he or she is never good enough, or that they have needs that are insatiable. That they are greedy and ugly and totally underserving of any love or care. This deeply shaming experience can leave a lasting wound that continues into adulthood and undermines a person's life. If this has happened to you, it is time to send that shame back to where it came from. You were not to blame.

Shame and sexual abuse:

In particular, shame is an emotion that is very strong for people that may have been abused either mentally, emotionally, or physically. It is especially acute after sexual abuse. After abuse your body may feel dirty and you feel like you have been contaminated. For a child that has been abused sexually by a parent, it can be doubly so. It can also be very confusing. The child is torn between the need to be lovingly touched, to be protected by their carer, and the harm being done to them by that very person.'

What happens when the carer or parent is harming the child sexually or otherwise? Under normal circumstances, a child would run to their parent for protection. But now the parent is causing the harm. This kind of abuse can seriously affect the child's developing brain circuitry and leave them feeling an enormous amount of shame.

Whose shame is this?

The question is, what part of the shame is your experience, and what part is the shame of the abuser? For a small child that was sexually abused, they may feel that they brought this experience on themselves. Children that are sexually abused are often in a terrible compromise of trust and need. Above all they need love, physical care, and contact from their carers. They are hard wired to be cute and cuddly to encourage carers to fulfil their need for lots of physical contact. However, if this is contaminated with sexual contact, it might be hard to separate the need for care and contact from what was inappropriate sexual contact. The feeling of need can make them feel responsible for getting what they didn't need, the inappropriate behaviour. Especially when then they know how cute and beguiling they are; they then might feel ashamed for this.

Children can also become sexualised by inappropriate sexual contact, which means that they can also invite sexual contact. It can mean that it is much harder to have normal, connected, loving relationships; instead it becomes 'normalised' to seek out sexual relationships. Sex gets mixed up for love and the now-developing teenager can be much more vulnerable to further sexual abuse from the incestuous parents, siblings, family friends, or strangers. The majority of sexual abuse actually happens within the family system.

Whatever happened to you as a child was not your fault. Even in the event that you developed precocious sexuality and became promiscuous. This was all a consequence of what happened to you as a child.

It was the behaviour of the abuser towards you that was shameful. Even, and especially, if that abuser was a family member or your own parent. Your abuser was an adult and was responsible for his or her behaviour. An adult can never morally blame a child for what has happened. It would be an inexcusable thing to happen.

An adult is the teacher and the leader. It is never the child that is responsible, no matter what happened. It is the role of the adult to care for the child. It is inappropriate for an adult to seek to satisfy their emotional or sexual needs through the child or to make the child bad or wrong when the adult's needs are not met. A traumatised adult with poor boundaries can very unconsciously exploit the innocence of a child and then project their own shame onto the child. The child will always believe that the adult's behavior is correct and that their own pain and suffering is wrong, That they are unloveable. This inappropriate molestation of a child, whether it is overt penetrative sex or 'grooming' and seduction of a child through the giving of presents, will always leave a child feeling bad or wrong in some way. It is the adult behavior that is wrong. If you find yourself as an adult drawn to these abuses, then seek help. If this happened to you as a child, you also need help to heal this abuse.

It is possible that the experience was so bad for you that you have also taken on your abusers' shame. Can you have some compassion for yourself?

Can you give the shame back?

How long have you been carrying this burden of pain? How has it affected your life? What are the lost opportunities that you have endured because you haven't felt worthy? Is this the way that you want to continue the rest of your life? Are you ready to give it back? Or have you identified with it for so long that it feels to be part of who you are?

If you have a 100% commitment to heal, this is an important decision to make.

The feeling of shame from abuse can plague not only a childhood victim, but also an adult who was abused in the form of rape and/or violence by a partner. Either way, it could be that you have taken on this shame because you hold yourself responsible for letting the shameful event happen. If you are feeling *'it was my fault, I should have said no,'* or *'I could have stopped it happening if I hadn't decided to go out with him'*, or *'I shouldn't have gone on my own'* or any one of those things. What does your shame voice say? Either way, there is nothing from your side to be shameful about.

Unfortunately, with abuse, the onus is often on the victim that they somehow caused the event to happen. How ridiculous! How many beaten wives have been told by their violent husbands, *'you made me hit you'*? It is quite plainly nonsense. Also, in law courts, it has been difficult to prove rape in the past because perpetrators say that they have been 'led on', this is another nonsense and is now changing. This societal bias and behaviour is also shameful. Are you going to carry this shame or give it back?

As well as the abuse that has happened personally, all women have 'gender' abuse happening on an ongoing basis. Varying levels of abuse and degradation towards women is considered acceptable on every continent, world-wide, by at least a portion of the populace — if not the majority. We ALL carry the shame of this situation, and it is a planetary work of healing to remove it. Both men and women will also be contaminated with this shame. I am not being feminist in saying this is happening to women, men also get sexually abused and bullied. It is about the abuse of the feminine principle also. Unfortunately, because women are identified with the 'feminine principle', they carry the largest part of the abuse. Men tend to identify with the 'masculine principle' but can be equally damaged when they try to express their feminine side. If you are a man or a woman not wanting to embody a negative masculine, then you may be attacked or abused. If you don't conform to the stereotypic norm — i.e. if you are gay, or if you are quiet and creative, you may be bullied. Luckily this is beginning to change. If you identify with any of these situations, you could be carrying shame that is not yours.

Shame that you got hurt

Another source of shame arises from not being able to avoid the situation that traumatised you. Humans go into parasympathetic shock when in extreme danger. This can prevent them from being able to run away, and they may later blame and shame themselves because of it; consider it their fault. They may think, "*if only I had hit back*" or "*if I had run away*" it wouldn't have happened. This is also the case when someone else is injured or killed, and we were unable to do anything to protect the other person. The reality is, that in those moments when our primitive brain puts us into parasympathetic shock and shuts down, we have no choice. We are made entirely limp and helpless as a survival mechanism. We cannot run away, and we cannot fight. We cannot save someone else when our nervous system has intervened in this way. We have totally lost the power of our legs and arms. We have become speechless with terror. When we recover and see what has happened, we take it upon ourselves. We blame and shame ourselves for being inadequate and failing. But it could not have happened differently in this moment.

Are you ready to let go of the shame?

Shame can be a challenging emotion to eradicate, especially since it also has a biological survival basis which makes us act small so that we are not seen. It causes us to feel defective, and we are then pushed out by our social group — or we take ourselves out. However, it can be healed; it is all about allowing ourselves to be seen, and by neutralising the corrosive voice of shame. Returning it to its source and taking the power out of it. Regaining our rightful place and connection to our self and our community.

If your life has been eaten away by shame and you are ready to put it in its place, here is another step that you can take to do this.

Exercise 16

Transforming your shame

For this exercise, you need to identify your shame statements again. You can either look at the shame packyou created, or you can write them down again. For each statement, it is important to write in calm and soothing language, much as you would for a small child or vulnerable person. This statement should refute the shame statement. For instance, if your shame statement is *"I am just a hopeless loser"*, you could counter it with *"you did your best and no-one else could have done any better"*. Make sure that you have a soothing statement for each shame statement. When you have done this, then it is important to stand in front of the mirror and see yourself. Make eye contact with yourself. Now tell yourself the soothing statements. When you have finished, tell yourself: *"I forgive myself for feeling this shame". "I love you"*. As you do this, notice how you feel in your body. What has changed? How has your posture changed? What has happened to your tone of voice? Write in your journal about what is different in the way that you feel physically, mentally, and emotionally. You may have to do this quite a few times. Keep practicing, and experience what happens. Work with yourself as you change, and support yourself through this difficult process with compassion.

When is the right time to Forgive?

It is said that the victim of abuse should forgive their abuser. It is thought that it is a healing process to do so. Whilst forgiveness is a powerful healing process, it is important that it happens appropriately and spontaneously from the heart, and is not a contrived and forced attempt to heal a situation. The reality is a little more complex. Genuine and deep forgiveness can only happen after the necessary healing of the wounded person has taken place.

For a child or vulnerable person who was abused, it is a further abuse to offer forgiveness when there has been no recognition of the suffering that they have been through. It is not the role of someone who was sexually abused as a child, to now become the 'adult' and forgive the abuser. There needs to be an interim period when that abused person really deeply builds compassion for their self and the suffering that they have been through. When they have done this, then they can move to the next step of finding compassion for their abuser.

Forgiving the abuser before this has taken place is like sealing a wound which is still infected and the pus is underneath the scab. It is not possible to forgive someone who has done you harm when you have not healed the damage that was done to you. The first step is to take care of yourself, and to really acknowledge how painful the situation was for you. Acknowledge and truly see how much suffering it caused you; how it has undermined your life and your sense of self.

Witness for yourself all the secondary traumatisation where people judged you because you were not able to 'step up to the mark' and perform in the way that they thought you should. Understand how the abuse may have prevented you from being able to pay attention in school and impaired your learning. Comprehend how it could have affected your ability to feel safe in a relationship and caused you to make bad choices in love relationships. See all the bullying that may have happened as a result of how your capacity to relate with skillful boundaries was impaired by the abuse. You need to really be aware of all the details of how you have embodied and been shaped by the experience of abuse. In this way, you can put the blame and shame back where it belongs. You can begin to understand that you are

NOT an intrinsically bad and shameful person that has screwed up all your life. You are the way that you are because of the abusive environment that you grew up in. You were shaped by that abuse. You had to find a way to live through it; to survive as best as you could.

Don't relive the past

In doing this reckoning with the past and understanding how it shaped you, it does not mean that you have to go back and relive the past. You don't have to churn up every story and grueling episode of what you went through. It's about understanding how it has shaped you. Instead, seek the effects of the past in the present. Where are the parts of your life that are not working for you? Can you begin to understand how you made choices when being abused, in order to survive and feel safe? I mean, how have you been living your life SINCE the time of the abuse and what do you need to change NOW to be whole again?

What was your total loss? Was it a loss of innocence? Was it a loss of trust? Or of love? How did it cause you to cut off from connection, and how did it cause you take on the shame? Before you can forgive, you need to go through an emotional audit and, from that position, the focus is on healing the loss through grieving.

What are the emotions that you have been burying

What are the other emotions that you are holding as a result of the harm caused to you? Maybe, as well as grief, there is sadness, resentment, pessimism, regret, hatred, anger, rage? Have you had to keep a lid on such feelings throughout your life, thus feeling crippled by the intensity... of keeping it all together, being careful not to let it spill out on to the children or anyone else that you are close to?

Have you been unable to really attend to what you wanted to in life because of it? Does it feel that your life has been one really long-lost opportunity, and you have had endless cycles of the same thing happening over and over, until you are not sure that you even want to go on living? It is time to own up to these feelings and take care of yourself because of them. Acknowledge them. It can be a challenging but worthwhile process. Take it slowly, and trust your body. One baby step at a time. Learn to build compassion for yourself by practicing loving-kindness on a daily basis. Gently encourage the inner critic to rest and let go. Tell yourself that you are really sorry that it has all happened to you, but you love yourself and are there for yourself. Support yourself in this healing process. Little by little these other complex emotions can subside and heal. Use the tools being shown you here to help you, especially the ones that teach you to be more connected to your bodily sensations. Build more resources in your life to support you and when you need it, reach out for professional help.

In order to heal it is important for you to be in the driving seat of your life.

You need now to show up and take responsibility for your life by really understanding the emotions that you have been allowing to colour your experience day by day. The past is over and done with.

The past is finished unless you choose — by not acting — to let it keep running in the present.

It may be hard to 'show up' and take control of your life because of the intensity of feelings or because you are in such a deeply frozen or overwhelmed shocked state, but this can heal — especially with the tools and approach that I am teaching here. Human beings are remarkable in their power and their capacity to heal. You are one of these remarkable human beings. Just like all the others you can do what is necessary to heal your life.

Allow yourself to grieve:

As you begin to do this emotional audit of what happened to you, and how it has affected your life, you may feel grief for all the loss that you identify. It is normal that you should feel a great deal of sadness. Grieving is a universal experience that we go through in relationship to loss. Loss can come in many different forms. It can be the loss of a loved one, or a home, or identification with a particular life-style. It can be a loss of one's innocence and everything that this has entailed, as previously mentioned.

It is important, in this grieving process, to allow the sadness to happen. Don't try to block it out or suppress it. Let it flow. Resisting the feelings of grief or pushing them down will only prolong the pain. It will pass when you have allowed its full expression. Don't beat yourself up for having these feelings; support yourself through it with kindness. Eventually, you will come to a point of acceptance of what has happened. With acceptance can come grace that can settle on your life. You will then be in a position to transform the pain and use it to build a new life.

You have the power to heal.

YOU CAN DO IT!

By taking account of all the things in your life that were affected by the abuse, and grieving the loss, you come to a new understanding of yourself. When this true audit has happened, you can then witness the growth that you have made that has transformed this old situation. Perhaps you can find what it was that helped you get through all the pain. What was it in you that supported your survival? Was there a person who was able to support you in some way? Or was there something special that you found that helped you through, such as an animal or a connection with nature? Something somewhere helped you through this situation. See if you can feel the connection to this still. Can you identify that part of yourself that was resilient and helped you through? Can you connect again to those resources — the power of nature, or the unconditional love of an animal or friend — that helped you through? If you can do this, you are on the way to transforming the pain.

Supporting your inner child:

One way that you can help yourself in this healing journey is to support yourself through reaching out and taking care of your inner child. This could not only be about healing from abuse, but also any other scary or hurtful experience that you had when you were little.

Imagine this small child that was you, standing or sitting in front of you. Reach out and pick him or her up and tell the little one that you are now here to listen to the way he or she suffered. You are NOW READY to show up and take of him or her, and nothing like it will ever happen again. Imagine holding the little one really closely and lovingly. You can do this in a meditation or just take the time to sit down and talk with your younger self. You can take her or him with you wherever you go and really include the little one in what you are doing. It is time to heal the loneliness. It has been a time of enormous fear, carrying all the pain for so long. Your inner child needs all your love and reassurance.

Your little one may not just be sad because of abuse; it could be any unpleasant occurrence which shouldn't happen to a child. Perhaps your Mum or Dad died, or you lost a sibling. Even if this happened before your birth, it still might have had a profound impact upon you. Perhaps you were bullied and no one stood up for you? Perhaps you witnessed violence? Maybe you were in a bad catastrophe or an accident? Perhaps you were very ill and hospitalised for a long time, or had some really distressing surgery? Perhaps you were in a war zone, or are a refugee? Maybe everyone around you was so stressed by the bad things that were happening, that they didn't really look out for you? Now is the time to heal this.

The above process of witnessing yourself may take lots of time. It is important to give it as much time as it needs. New waves of feeling might come up. Always be ready with love and acceptance for yourself, and offer yourself a helping hand of kindness. Learn to be deeply compassionate towards yourself. Gradually, your inner child will feel safer and that will translate to you as an adult. You will feel more at ease in life and happier.

Compassion:

Developing compassion is the surest way of creating lasting happiness for yourself.

Compassion is the total empathic acceptance of the suffering of someone else or yourself. It comes from the heart, and is developed by a continual practice of choosing to be compassionate. It is the highest principle, and the most powerful healing energy. It often takes a person a long time to feel self-compassionate. First of all, it is necessary to work through all the self-judgement, blame, and shame.

Then it is about truly seeing how you have suffered, and be willing to be kind and loving towards yourself. Finally, you can begin to build self-compassion.

Are you willing and ready to have compassion for yourself and what you went through?

It is not possible to be compassionate towards anyone else if you don't know how to do it for yourself. It may be difficult at first, but it is important to learn. Stop being self-critical and feeling that it is all your fault and that you are 'useless'; have some understanding for yourself and the difficult challenges that you have been through. Take time every day to say to yourself, *'I am really sorry about what you went through. I really love you and will take care of you now.'* Look at yourself in the mirror, look in youreyes and say *'I love you'*. If there is resistance to that, notice it and explore what that is about. It is so important in the healing process to love oneself and to have self-compassion.

The healing force is generated by you, towards yourself, and for yourself. If you are self-critical, how can you heal? Can you recognise how self-judgement and criticism is a barrier to true healing? Instead, be gentle and allow self-compassion to grow. Once you have established this for yourself, then it is a natural continuation to be able to be compassionate towards others, even those people who have done you harm.

Releasing the pain with forgiveness and love:

As you become more compassionate, and accepting of what has happened to you, your healing can turn towards releasing the pain with forgiveness and love. This is not necessarily the forgiveness of the perpetrator of your suffering, but it might eventually become so. First of all, it is about self-forgiveness. Can you forgive yourself for what you feel you did to cause such a situation? It could be that you need to forgive even choosing to be born. Go as deep as you need to whenever the pain comes up. You can say, *'I release this with forgiveness and love'*. When you are doing your somatic experiencing and mindfulness meditations, and you touch on the painful areas, hold them in your awareness, breath into them and say, *'I release this with forgiveness and love'*. Little by little things will begin to change.

As time goes by, you may even reflect on the person or the situation that caused you to be harmed; you may even feel that God let you down. If there is an impulse from the heart to do so — and only in that instance — you can forgive that person or situation. *'I forgive you for what happened'*. IT IS IMPORTANT THAT THIS STEP IS NEVER FORCED. It may never happen that you do this, but if you do come to this point naturally, then it may be very healing. It may feel like a sense of grace has descended upon your life and blessed you; enabling you to move forward and truly let go of the past, even at an emotional level.

Finding the gold in your experience:

As the pain and the trauma heals, you will experience more spaciousness in your being. You will have more ability to reflect rather than react. As your life opens up, and you begin to grow in ways that you never expected or anticipated, you may begin to appreciate that the negative experiences were the soil and fertiliser for the **new you**. You could not be who you are now if these things had not happened to you. Be aware of how much of the depth of your being, your compassion and understanding, were born out of the suffering that you went through. See how the particular skills that you have were honed in the fires of your distress. How were your coping strategies transformed into gifts for developing your life? Everything can be transformed, and there can be gold under every stone that you turn in your life. Even if you are not at this point yet, know that it can happen. Begin to practice it even, when you are having a difficult day; imagine how you can use the experience that you are currently having in order to improve your awareness and understanding of life and other people's experiences.

Perhaps, as you disentangle from the bad situation, you may consider a new career direction or a new occupation, using the wisdom of your experience. It is very common that people who have been through intensely difficult and painful situations, turn them around to be of service to others. This is certainly what I have done in my life. My experiences have given me extraordinary insight into the suffering of others, as well has given the capacity and the compassion to help them. I know many people who have had really challenging experiences, and who then use themto become an 'expert' to help others with the same thing. This is the inner alchemy that is possible for all of us as spiritual beings on planet earth. We are born, we suffer, we transform our suffering, and we grow. We help others to grow.

Finding your mission:

What is it that you **could do** now?

How can you use what happened to become fired up with a passion to help others in some way, or to change something so that this does not happen again?

Are you ready and willing to step into a **new you** that is proactive, and wanting to live life to the fullest possible degree?

I firmly believe that each one of us came to this planet, and incarnated in this human body, for a purpose. We each have a mission to fulfil.

In Buddhist teachings, they say that a human life is a precious thing; that on the wheel of incarnation and rebirth, it is only when we finally incarnate as a human being that we can have the right conditions to advance our soul's evolution. The soul grows when it is able to move from experiencing and embodying the grosser emotional elements into the higher principles.

Anger, greed and lust — for instance — are lower, whilst love, kindness, and compassion are higher. Can you now also see this as a possible evolutionary step for yourself? In this respect, your life has been a unique opportunity to be able to develop these qualities.

Are you willing and ready to consciously embrace such a possibility?

It is a unique opportunity to have a human birth:

In embryological terms, it is extremely difficult to get born as a human being. The chances are against you making it — from the stage of being an egg or a sperm, through to conception, implantation, then growing and thriving in the womb, and finally getting born alive as a human being.

To have achieved this you are a winner. Billions of sperm die on the way towards the egg. Hundreds of eggs die after ovulation. It is a unique occasion for an egg and a sperm to meet up and to join together in conception. It is an incredible moment of possibility.

This happened to you.

For the blastocyst to make the perilous journey down the fallopian tube without dying on the way, is another remarkable event. You made it! You survived! Then there is implantation in your Mother's womb, another developmental stage that may be fraught with difficulty. You succeeded this one as well! Then to grow and develop into the incredible being that is you, was a magnificent achievement! Then came birth. Birth is harder than death. It is quite an ordeal, yet you made it through that as well! You are indeed a winner! This needs a really big celebration. Celebrate yourself and your life.

For you, as a soul, to choose to go through all this meant that you had a desire, an impulse, to be here. You had a mission that you were on, and you are still traveling on that path. You went through some really challenging — and many life-threatening — experiences along the way and you survived them all. The seed of that mission is carried deeply within you and has always been there, slowly germinating in the soil of all your experiences.

YOU SURVIVED:

Full consciousness is when you wake up to the reality of who you truly are at a soul level. You have been through a huge amount of darkness which has obscured the true you. By shining a light on your experiences in your emotional healing, you have begun to be in touch with the true you. Take time to really celebrate this awareness that YOU HAVE SURVIVED. You have come through all the challenges. You are an immensely powerful person with an amazing ability to create your life, moment by moment. Well done! It is time — when you are ready — to turn your creative abilities towards that which will bring benefit and happiness to you. The past is over, and there is only the present moment which is full to brimming with extraordinary potential.

As I sit writing this, I am noticing a rose outside my window, battered yesterday with hail stones and heavy rain. Now the sun is shining and illuminating the raindrops hanging from the petals. They shine with a brilliance and intensity, capturing and scattering the light of the sun in a myriad of directions.

You, too, have been through the storms, and the sun is shining again. Now, as you capture the light, where will it be directed too? You don't have to do anything but allow your brilliance to shine.

You have taken the deep, painful charge out of the wounding caused by the abuse or the traumatic experience. You are now in a position to truly forgive.

Ho'oponopono

Ho'oponopono (ho-o-pono-pono) is an ancient Hawaiian practice of reconciliation and forgiveness. Similar forgiveness practices were performed on islands throughout the South Pacific, including Samoa, Tahiti, and New Zealand.

It can be used for anything in your life; any difficult and challenging situation. It is about understanding that everything in the universe is a part of you, and that there is an interconnectedness that you can use to influence for the good of everyone and everything. By being the point of consciousness that is intending harmony and well-being — through a practice of repentance, gratitude, forgiveness, and love — you affect a change; it is also useful for harmonising relationships.

This simple practice was used by a therapist who cured every patient in the criminally insane ward of a Hawaii State Hospital — without ever seeing a single patient. It's not a joke. The therapist was Dr Ihaleakala Hew Len. He reviewed each of the patients' files, and then he healed them by healing himself. Below is the practice, and it is called Ho'oponopono.

How to Practice Ho'oponopono in Four Simple Steps:

Repentance: I'm Sorry

This is the first step, and it doesn't mean that you are taking responsibility for the bad thing that happened. It means that you are sorry that it happened. We can all be sorry when something bad has happened either to ourselves or others.

You can do this exercise firstly for things that you know that you are responsible for in some way. For instance, being unkind to yourself. Draw the event to mind, see yourself and say, "I am sorry".

You can then do the exercise by meditating on the difficulty and, if there is another person involved, draw that person to mind and say "I am sorry that this has happened".

You can then add — if appropriate, and you would like to — an extra amount of self-responsibility. "I realise that I am responsible for the (issue) in my life, and I feel remorse that something in my consciousness has caused this."

Forgiveness: Please forgive me

Feel the repentance from step 1 and say "Please forgive me" You can repeat it over several times.

> Remember that in trauma terms, if you have unresolved trauma around being abused in any way, you should never be seeking forgiveness from your abuser.

Gratitude: Thank you

This act of 'Giving Thanks' can be directed at anything. It can be to your body for supporting you and making your life possible, for your friends that help you, for your heart beating — anything. Find a way to say thank you — in a strong, heartfelt way — for the space that you are in now.

Love: I Love You.

Finally, you say *"I love you"*. It can be to yourself, or it can be to the other person, persons, or events that you are working with. Say it to your body; to the air that you breath. Say *"I love you"* to your challenges. Embrace everything with an open and loving acceptance.

Extending this Exercise to the Ancestors:

If you are working with either yourself or another person, you can also work with ancestors. You can initially go to the mother and father and then further back. You can say *"I am truly sorry that this thing has happened"* *"Please forgive me"* *"Thank you"* *"I love you"*. You can work back and back — all the way to the earliest emergence of your lineage— and clear the whole line.

CHAPTER 6

Things to support your healing further

If you have read this far, you will have discovered that trauma is a complex experience which is characterised by a tendency for your primitive brain to go into a high level of activation as a result of being triggered by experiences that are not normally a threat. This instability of the nervous system gives rise to all sorts of symptoms on an emotional and physical level. The primary means of healing trauma is a therapy modality that has a body centred approach. This can be backed up with lots of activities that also engage the body. The primary requirement is that those activities are enjoyable, and build a sense of well-being in the body. In addition to this, 'Developmental Trauma' is much more complex, and requires very skilled support from specialists in trauma healing that can also offer psychotherapeutic work alongside the somatic skills that they can offer, i.e. body-based psychotherapy. In either event, it is important for the person suffering from trauma to have the caring support of friends and family, or another caring network of people. Above all, to heal from trauma, it is necessary to be committed to make the changes possible. If you have got this far in your life, something must have been working for you that you can now draw upon to help you further. We explored this a little bit in the previous chapter!

It is entirely possible to recover from trauma; there is lots of help for you.

Not only are there the approaches that I have described above, but other approaches and things to consider that will support your healing process. First and foremost, you must be really willing and committed to healing, and ready to embrace the help that there is. Often, when you have been really traumatised and incredibly lonely for a long time, it is hard to trust, or to believe that anything can help you. You may also have a pattern of not being able to reach out, and a disbelief that you will be welcomed by those who say they are there to help you. It is really important that you become conscious of patterns which might keep you stuck. Begin to notice where you are not moving forward as a result of attachment to the old way of being. It is now necessary to engage in the practical help that is available, and for certain you will heal.

What I describe below are easy, simple steps that you can take on your own that will begin to change the way things are for you.

EFT:

One very simple approach to tackling the emotional stumbling block described above, is to use the simple and totally free technique of EFT or Emotional Freedom Technique. It may at first seem complex to learn but if you follow the instructions on the chart and there are also many great YouTube videos to help guide you through, following these you will find it remarkably simple.

EFT has been developed from acupuncture and kinesiology, two very effective treatment methods. It works on the energy meridians and helps you to release difficult emotions. It is so effective that it has been used to heal the victims of genocide in Rwanda very successfully. It is also used in the Corporate world as a means of instilling more confidence into marketing and business development personnel.

EFT Tapping Points

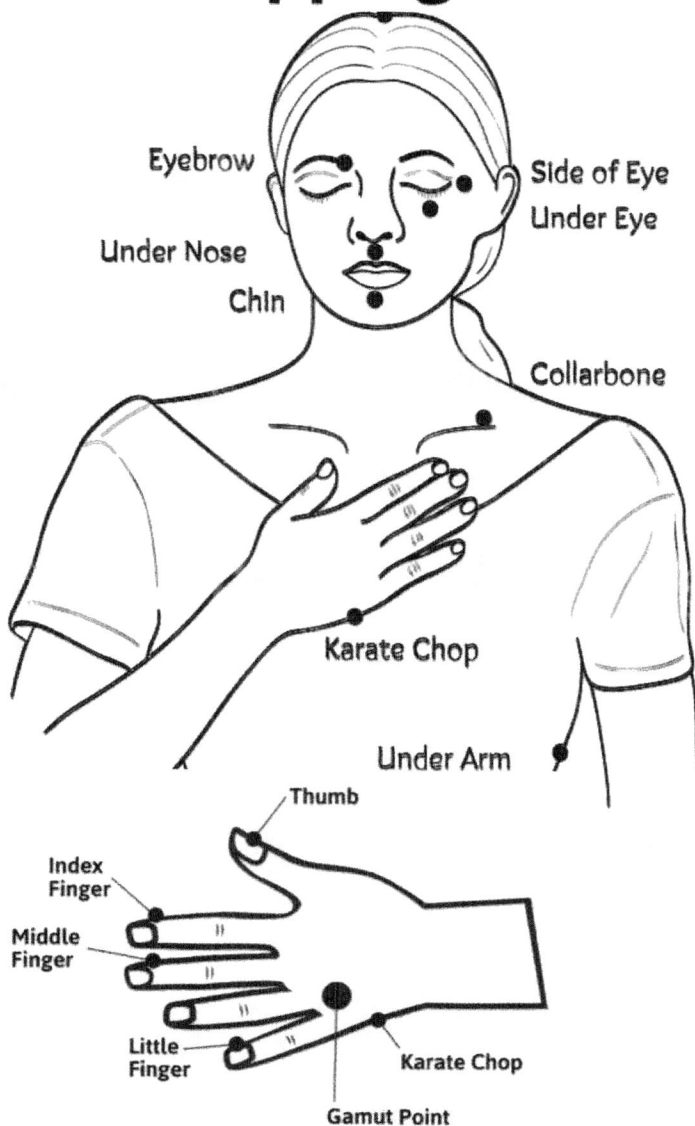

Eyebrow

Side of Eye

Under Eye

Under Nose

Chin

Collarbone

Karate Chop

Under Arm

Thumb

Index Finger

Middle Finger

Little Finger

Karate Chop

Gamut Point

How to use EFT

Anytime you identify a feeling that is blocking you, you can use EFT to move through it and release it. Perhaps you are frightened to ask for help? If that is the prevailing emotion of the moment you can work on this one. As you continue over time, you may find different emotions.

Although there are slight variations to the process, one way to do it is to begin by taking your right hand and place it on your chest on the left-hand side above the breast and below the collar bone. You are feeling with your fingers into the chest for something described as the 'sore point'. You might notice it a little tender there. When you find it, or even if you can't find it, just gently press that point and say, "Even though I am frightened to ask for help, I love and accept myself". You do this three times.

You now begin the tapping process. You tap lightly about seven times repeating the statement or holding the essence of it in your mind. Firstly, you tap on the points on either the left-hand or right-hand side of your body, in this order:

- ❖ Beginning of the eyebrow near the bridge of the nose.
- ❖ End of the eyebrow and outside edge of the eye.
- ❖ Under the eye
- ❖ Under your nose above the top lip.
- ❖ In the middle under your bottom lip.
- ❖ Under your collar bone, close to the centre.
- ❖ Under your armpit in line with your nipple.
- ❖ On the outside edge of your nail on your thumb.
- ❖ In the same place on your first finger.
- ❖ In the same place on your middle finger.

- ❖ Opposite side of your ring finger.
- ❖ In the same place on your little finger.
- ❖ On the karate chop point of your hand

Now you have to 'fix' the process with the Gamut Point.

With your left hand, feel into the webbing between your first and second fingers of your right hand. As you are pressing gently, do this process.

Look to your right, now roll your eyes around.

Look to your left, now roll your eyes around.

Count to five.

Hum a tune for a few seconds.

Count to five again.

Now repeat the tapping process on the right-hand side of your body repeating your statement or the essence of it.

You don't have to fix it again after this.

You might find that you yawn and release after doing the tapping. If, after going through this process once, the same feelings come up, you can use the simplified EFT routine. However, you don't always have to do the whole process, but do it the first time with that specific emotional issue. Once set up, it is advisable to do the simplified version frequently until it clears for you. This time, you can just tap on the karate point of your hand whilst repeating this statement. "Even though I (add in the experience that you are stuck with) I love and accept myself". You don't need to go through the whole process again and set it up each time.

Having done this, it doesn't mean that fear will never come up again, but it means that gradually it's hold over you will decrease. You will have more confidence to reach out. If you find that, after you have worked with the fear, another emotion is there, then work with that. If you feel you have done the tapping and nothing has changed, then tap on that. *"Even though it feels that nothing is changing, I love and accept myself"*. Repeat this as often as is necessary. Whilst doing this, maintain a high level of hydration. Have a glass of water at the same time to support the changes that are happening in your body.

EFT, once learnt, becomes a quick and easy method to use whenever you come up against difficult emotions. It can be very easily integrated into other things you are doing. It can also be very discreet. For instance, imagine that you are attending an interview, or are with someone who is challenging you, and a fear comes up that you have previously worked on and done the set up for, such as *"I don't feel good enough"*, you can quite easily — without it being noticed — tap the karate point on the side of your hand whilst repeating: *"Even though I don't feel good enough, I love and accept myself"*. Once. you have established the routine, it is powerful and effective even when you are just imagining doing it.

Cross Crawling:

One of the common symptoms of trauma is feeling unfocused and out of the body. This exercise helps ground you and re-establish clear focus. Cross Crawling works to integrate the left and right side of your brain. When the two sides of your brain are better integrated, it means that you are more able to do cognitive tasks (thinking, planning, and analytical). It is particularly helpful for conditions such as dyslexia, and is also used to help heal brain damage.

Cross crawling can help you be more focussed and feel more 'present', all important factors when healing from trauma, and especially from a dissociative tendency. It will help to lower your reactivity levels when you have been triggered by something, so it is also a wonderful resource.

It is fun to do, and you can do it just for a few minutes every day, or as and when you feel like it. It is a good to do when you are feeling ungrounded or activated. You can do it to music as well, which is a bonus unless you are sound sensitive. You can also make it fun by doing it as a dance.

It is best done standing; however, if you are physically unable to stand, you can still incorporate some of the moves in a sitting posture.

How to Cross Crawl:

The process of cross crawling is to move your arms and legs in unison, in a pattern. You move your limbs across the midline of your body, to touch limbs on the opposite side of your body. After a minute of doing this then you touch the limbs on the same side of your body.

For the first minute, you make movements across your body from the right to the left and from the left to the right. You can choose to make contact between various parts of the body. For instance, your hand on your knee, your hand on your shoulder, or your hand on your heel.

You move your right hand to touch your left knee and your left hand to touch your right knee. You do the same process, moving across your body to touch your shoulder on the opposite side. Then you move across your body to touch your foot on the opposite side and then your heel. You can do it in any order you like and for as long as you like.

You then change to make movements and connections on the same side of the body, so your right hand touches your right knee, then your shoulder, then your foot, then your heel. Your left hand now does the same with the parts of the body on the left side. After you have done this for a minute or so you switch back to touching the opposite sides of the body.

Arm and Leg Twists:

I don't know the actual name of this exercise so I hope that you can follow my instructions. However, you will find it if you search the term "Brain Gym' in YouTube and you might see this particular one. It works in a similar way to cross-crawling. You can do this standing or sitting. If you do it standing, it will also help you with balance.

Stretch both arms out in front of you and wrap them around each other. Then bend them at the elbows and bring your hands close to your face. Extend your thumb and touch yourself between the eyebrows on your 'third eye' which is also the starting point of your nervous system at the ethmoid bone. Spend thirty to sixty seconds breathing into this, then release and extend your arms again. Wrap them around each other in a different direction and bring your hands to touch the 'third eye' again.

The next stage of this process is to do the same thing with your legs (except that you don't bring your feet to touch your face!).   This will dramatically improve your balance. Wrap one leg around the other so that you are now standing on one foot. Hold this for at least thirty seconds. Now release and do it back the other way. When you have achieved your balance with the legs, then bring in the arm movement again so that you are now holding the complete posture.

Yoga:

Yoga is a group of physical, mental, and spiritual practices that originated from India. There are various styles of yoga but Hatha Yoga is possibly the one that would help you most if you have been unwell, since it is quite gentle.

Dr Bessel van der Kolk, one of the world's leading experts on Trauma Healing, highly recommends yoga as a means of healing trauma; it is soothing and calming, and integrates body and mind activities. You have to focus on what you are doing when you are engaged in yoga exercises. You cannot do it whilst your mind is wandering. It is deeply relaxing yet builds concentration, and also improves your health and your flexibility. Each yoga posture benefits your body and your metabolism in a different way. It is easy to do the simplest postures, and, as you become more flexible, you can do the more complex postures. If you research, you can probably find a class near you. It is very helpful to begin with a professional teacher, to ensure you find the right posture and appropriate practice for your ability level. You can also find yoga classes on YouTube and for many people this is a good way to do it.

Dancing:

Dancing is a wonderful way to heal. It gets your body moving to a rhythm, and helps you co-ordinate your movement. It is also fun and a way to engage socially. Dancing with a partner is especially helpful as this also builds relationship skills, and co-ordination between two people. Group dancing can be very soothing, such as Sufi dancing and Dances of Universal Peace; Bulgarian or Baltic dancing can be a bit more energetic and great fun. There is also a kind of dancing called Five Rhythms, developed by Gabrielle Roth, which is much more free form, with different tempo and mood music in five different phases. Dancing at home, whenever you feel like it, lifts the mood, exercises the body, and gets the endorphins flowing, helping you to feel happier.

Physical exercise of any kind is good for you.

Above, I have described a few examples of physical exercises that can be helpful in the healing of trauma. There are more that you could be doing. You could look for a class in any of those already suggested, or try energy exercises, such as Tai Chi, Chi Neng, Aikido, Kick Boxing etc. Walking, swimming, cycling, or gardening are all beneficial. They all help you get out of the house and engage in nature in some way. The list is long, and when you are able, it would be of great benefit to do something that is not over-stimulating, but soothing and grounding, and also brings you into social connection with others.

Exercise 17

Writing a Release Letter

As you become more grounded, with a greater understanding of your emotional process — and you've created a perception of yourself as witness to past events that are no longer controlling your life — you can do a little more emotional work to help you move on from the past.

One of these things is to write a letter sharing your feelings about hurt that was done to you. As you do your emotional processing, you may have one particular person that stands out that you have 'unfinished business' with. Or it could be a parent that hurt you in some way; or a partner that caused you harm. It could also be someone that you loved and lost through death, divorce, or an accident.

It is about someone with whom you shared some kind of experience which was not fully resolved. You may feel stuck in hurt feelings, or sadness, or anger with this particular person. Or it could be grief. You could even address such a letter to a circumstance, a set of events, or even God if you have a sense of being let down by the Divine.

When you are ready, set up a quiet, reflective space for yourself where you know you won't be disturbed. Perhaps light a candle. Have a pen and paper with you. Make sure that you are comfortable and fully resourced.

Sit and come into an awareness of your body and your breath. Bring to mind the unresolved situation or person which still carries upsetting feelings. Breathe into the memory and allow feelings to come up around that person or event. Witness the feelings; allow the thoughts of what you would have liked to have said at the time of the event, to come to mind.

Now write this all down, addressing the letter to the person or event by name. Allow yourself to write as much as flows. If you feel that you have finished, sit with it, breathe, and softly ask yourself, *'is there anything else that I need to express here?'* Breathe gently whilst you wait to see if there is anything else that wants to come up.

Give yourself plenty of time for this process so that you can really explore all the feelings that you have around this experience with the person (or event). Don't hold anything back. You are not going to send this letter. It is simply a way of saying all those things that you couldn't say at the time.

Since you have been doing your healing work, you have become a lot more aware of what happened to you, and what the hurt was. You have also become aware of how your life has been affected. Write it all down. Get it out and onto the paper. When you are totally finished, sign your name and fold the letter. Then fold the letter up and put it away in a safe place. Now go for a walk and move your body. Make sure that you fully resource yourself.

This letter writing may have been quite stirring, so give yourself lots of time and space to let this settle. Also be very kind to yourself. Don't judge yourself or be harsh to yourself. There is another stage to this process that you will be able to do once you have processed your emotions from this part.

"The release letter was to my ex-husband asking for peaceful reconciliation of our divorce settlement for me and my five sons (hence the seven hearts). There was a lot of anger in our relationship, and the intention was to transform the yang fire (of anger) into yin fire (a candle symbolising hope and peace). We are now in mediation to resolve the issue."It is entirely possible to recover from trauma; there is lots of help for you."

Rachel Elnaugh

Exercise 18

Creating a ritual with your letter

The next stage is to do something with the letter that symbolises a 'letting go' or 'release of the experience', and the intention to now move forward into your life. There are any number of things that you can do and they all involve disposing of the letter. Some suggestions are:

◇ Burn the letter

◇ Shred the letter and scatter it into some moving water

◇ Bury the letter and plant an acorn, or some other seed or plant over it, symbolising transformation and new growth.

You have a powerful and creative mind; it is for you to create your unique ritual.

You may also want to write an intention for healing before doing the ritual, so that you can state it clearly at the end. You may want to get in touch with the intention in the same, meditative, way as you did with writing the letter. Let your intention be as big and as strong as you want to make it. Do not limit it in any shape or form. This is a powerful commitment, through your imagination and creative powers, to direct yourself on the best life path that you possibly can. Now write it down on a piece of paper to keep; you might even like to frame it.

Prepare to do the ritual at a significant time, day, moon phase, or special point of remembrance — or even later in the same day if you feel well enough resourced, and have processed the feelings expressed in the letter. Set a clear intention in your mind of what you are about to do. Make sure that you are not under any time pressure, and you won't be disturbed. Make sure you will be warm and comfortable and fully present to the experience of the ritual. Afterwards, state your intention for how you want your life to be healed now that you've let go. When you have finished this, congratulate yourself and do something to celebrate. Notice how you feel in your body as a result of what you have done. What feels different now? Write down your experience of these two exercises. What was helpful? What was difficult? Maybe there is someone, or something, else that you also would like to write a letter to? Give it some time and space before you embark upon the next one.

"The release letter transformation exercise was particularly poignant as I burnt the letter and mixed it with clay. I made the clay + ashes mix into a tea-light holder, surrounded with seven hearts, which I painted gold and placed as a centrepiece on the kitchen table. Every day for a year, I lit a candle in it. Then a house guest decided to 'borrow it' for a shamanic ceremony without realising it was anything important and it ended up in the hands of someone else who was attending the event. At first I was angry but quickly realised that the healing was now complete - so I asked her to bury it in her garden."
- Rachel Elnaugh

Spend a few days being self-aware; notice how are your feelings are changing. Notice if you have dreams about it, or whether your dreams are changing. Notice what turns up in your life. Your external life is usually a reflection of what is going on at an inner level.

Exercise 19

Practicing Gratitude

The simple practice of gratitude is profoundly helpful when reframing the suffering caused by trauma. When your mind has been running for years on how much your life has been undermined by what has happened to you, it can become very negative. Chronic negative thinking can affect your hormones, your body posture, and the way you feel about life. It becomes a self-fulfilling prophesy. Life brings you what you think it will. If you think everything is bad and fearful, that is the way you will perceive it, so that is the way it will be, for you. However, to have a better life, you need to break out of the loop of negative thinking.

It can be hard to think about your life any differently when all you have known is pain, but it is possible. It is like building a muscle. Start to turn your mind around, and everything will begin to follow.

Reflect on things in your life that you take for granted. What does your life depend upon? What would it be like if you didn't have those things? What are you grateful for?

Consider your ability to talk, see, hear, move around, even breath easily. Without these sensory experiences, life is very different. Even if you have an impairment in, or loss of, some of these capabilities, there are many other things to be grateful for.

As well as these fundamental abilities that we take for granted, what other gifts do you have? Things that you can do, like reading and writing, maybe playing an instrument, painting, other craft skills? Perhaps language skills, or sports abilities? Sewing, knitting, cooking? We are all gifted with lots of abilities. What are you able to do that you have never really thought of as being anything special?

We also mainly have many basic possessions that we don't appreciate? Do you have a home? Running water, heat, and food? Items of clothing, shoes, books perhaps, a car maybe? What other personal items do you have that are of value to you? By value, I don't mean that they have a high financial value, but they make your life easier in some way. Where would you be without the simplest of things like a cup and saucer? Things, so often, taken for granted.

And our relationships? Is there anyone you're grateful to have in your life? A child, a partner, a sibling, or parents. Or maybe some good friends? A mentor? Or maybe someone who has inspired you? Someone who made a difference to your life? Perhaps not even a person you know, but a stranger you may have passed on the street one day who said something that changed your life!

The point is, that there are things in your life which, if you thought about it, you would appreciate how much they have enriched your life. Think carefully about it; imagine how it would be without those things and people in your life. Can you see how your life is so much better, in so many ways, by people and possessions that you currently don't notice or value?

Even if you can't find anything amongst all those suggestions, can you feel gratitude for the air that you breath, or the earth that supports your feet? The flowers that brighten your day, or maybe the birds that sing outside your window? If you can't think of anything, then begin to look out for those things, those little experiences that somehow brighten your life. The raindrops falling on the window pane. The magic of the wind blowing the leaves on an autumn day. Scarlet skies as the sun sets. The slim, silvery, crescent moon, rising in the night sky. What is your favourite nature experience? The sound of the waves crashing on the shore, or the hiss of the receding water back through the sands to the sea?

Finding gratitude for life is a practice that will make a huge difference to your mood, and your feelings about yourself.

Upon waking each morning, it is really powerful to start to go through the inevitable long list of all that you have to be grateful for by saying: "I am so happy and grateful that I have the ability to do....." or "I am so happy and grateful that I have a nice place to live" or "that I have a warm, dry place to sleep" or "I have someone in my life that I love". "I am grateful for the sun that is shining today". I am grateful for waking and knowing that I am alive".

What happens for you if you don't feel grateful? You could choose to say

: "I choose to be happy and grateful". As you say these words, feel into your body, what does it feel like as you affirm the things that are good in your life? What are the sensations that you feel as you say those words? What begins to change in you as you practice this each morning upon waking?

Ceremony and Ritual:

Creating ceremony is another way to create specialness in your life and to make it worth living.

Ceremony is a wonderful way of getting into your unconscious mind and triggering it for a change. It is used in every spiritual tradition and is an ancient and integral part of human consciousness. The remains of the oldest ceremonial activities are dated at least as far back as 30,000 years during the Paleolithic era.

The archaeological remains are a testimony to how necessary and powerful ceremony is to human beings. Ceremony can be anything that you choose to make it. It can be a part of an organised religion or spiritual group, or it can be something that you do for yourself. In shamanic healing, ceremony and ritual is often used to heal trauma. In fact, Peter Levine says that shamanic rituals bear a striking resemblance to somatic healing.

You can choose to create rituals and ceremonies, unique to you, all the way through your healing trauma process. At this point, when you are considering the alchemy of transforming your experiences of trauma into something that will nurture your life, you can design a ceremony around that transformation process. One of the things that you can do is to create actions that symbolise a change from a previous state to the present desired state. So, for instance, with your letter that you may have written to a person that caused you suffering, you may have chosen to dispose of the letter in a way that symbolises letting go of the suffering and the attachment to that kind of relationship with the person in question. Did you choose to shred, burn, or bury, the letter? You might have aligned this ritual with a particular day that is meaningful for you in some way, such as a birthday, an anniversary of the traumatic event, or maybe a particular phase of the moon or an eclipse.

When creating a ritual or ceremony, you might want to take special objects that mean something to you and stimulate you to settle into a particular way of feeling, or create particular supportive feeling tones for you. They might be objects that you have had for a long time (related to particular situations), or they might be candles, crystals, flowers, or incense. When you have gathered your chosen items, set time aside for the ritual.

You can write special words to say, or sounds and songs to sing. All these things work together to create an altered state of consciousness more deeply connected with your subconscious mind; this facilitates shifts that you may not even be aware of. It might be a slow melting — deep within you — in your psyche, or your relational field with a particular person that eventually flowers into a more obvious shift in the circumstances. It can in due course become a change in the way that you relate to life and yourself.

After completing any ritual or ceremony, it is interesting to note how you feel different in your body. Give yourself some space to be quiet and reflect on how you feel. Go inward and tune in with your somatic awareness; you may feel some changes inside.

Celebration

Many years ago, in a workshop with Native American healer Jamie Sams, I was told to *"celebrate more than I mourn"*. It was good advice, and I have always tried to create that balance in my life. Celebration gives us energy; mourning depletes our energy. If we want to be well, then anything that is going to increase our available energy is beneficial. There are particular key points in our lives when it is a good idea to celebrate. For instance, you might celebrate after doing your 'letting go' ritual because you've freed yourself. By celebrating, you are strengthening the 'feeling tones' around letting go and transforming that which was painful in your life into something which will take your life in a better, more fulfilling direction.

Celebrating is like drawing a line under something to say: *"It is done!"* We often fail to celebrate; this can undermine our sense of success. It makes it harder for us to have a sense of progression and completion of a stage in our life's journey. With trauma — which in itself is a state of 'stuckness' — it is particularly important to get a sense of forward motion and progress. We need to know that we are moving away from that which was causing us suffering, and making headway to a new life.

When you celebrate it means you give power to the positive steps you have taken

When making a plan for transformation and healing, it will consist of a series of stages to reach a final goal. Each stage can be challenging and take a lot of determination to get through. To support yourself and to give yourself more power, you can have a small celebration upon completion of each stage, and then a larger celebration when you attain the final goal. A celebration can involve anything that gives you a sense of reward. It can be taking a walk after studying hard for a few hours. Or having a piece of chocolate. It could be a night out with some special friends, or a holiday.

Celebrations can be huge affairs or they can be small, private moments. Choose a celebration which is appropriate for each stage, and don't be shy to ask others to join you. Friends and family often like to share these precious moments with you. For those of us who have been especially traumatised early in life, celebration can feel exceptionally difficult, particularly around times like birthdays and major social occasions, such as Christmas.

These events can be loaded with other meanings that can be painful and make us want to shut down. Also, it often happens with trauma that when the nervous system tends to get triggered into anxiety, any kind of high energy can have the same affect. So, anxiety and excitement can be closely linked. As you get excited and in a happy mood, anxiety can start to happen. It's important to be aware of this and to pace yourself in these experiences. Practice celebrating in gentle ways and gradually you will be able to have pleasure without it turning into upset.

Re-create your own meaning for special times like birthdays and anniversaries, especially now that you are transforming your life. Start small, with private moments, and build up until you are ready to invite others in. Create a system of rewards that helps you to feel — in a whole-body way — that you have achieved a goal. If you have a tendency to be an over-achiever, then let yourself off the hook and give yourself small, easy goals and reward them well. If negative feelings come up, then you have the other tools such as EFT to work with them. For instance, *"Even though I don't feel that I have done anything worthwhile, I love and accept myself"*. Take time to write a list of the kind of things that you would like to do to celebrate. They need to be resourcing, but also special; things that you don't necessarily get to do all the time. Things that you can perhaps save up for, or take some special time out. Go on, you can do it!

Good diet:

They say that we are what we eat, and it is certainly true with regards to our health. If you have been under considerable stress for a long period of time, the chances are that your body is very depleted. When long term stress repeatedly floods your body with cortisol and adrenaline, it is very debilitating, and you need to take extra care with nourishment, especially since distressed or depressed people tend not to make the   effort to eat well. Unfortunately, the more 'run down' you are physically, then the less well you are likely to feel emotionally. When your physical health is poor, it is easy to feel that you are on an emotional 'roller coaster'. When your body is strong and healthy, then your emotions become healthy.

I am not going to discuss diet in depth here, it is covered in the sequel to this book, *"I Can Do It"*. However, whatever your food preferences, there are some basic guidelines to healthy eating. It doesn't have to be complicated; it is just about going back to basics with quality foods and good nutrition. Learn which foods are detrimental to your health, and those loaded with harmful ingredients which leave a toxic load in your body.

Eat Real Food:

Firstly, eat REAL food and not JUNK food. I know it might be a bit difficult if you are used to getting those 'all in a packet foods' that you can put in the microwave, or a can of food that you just open, but it is worth the effort. If you are 100% committed to your recovery and your health, you need to change habits now. But don't be hard on yourself, you may have developed these habits as a result of being very stressed and did not realise how much your health could be compromised by poor nutrition. It is not too late to change, and your health and stress levels will improve dramatically with proper nutritional care. You will feel more at ease in your body, with way more energy and a feeling of well-being, besides being much more emotionally stable.

Buy Organic Food:

Secondly, buy organic food whenever you can. The nutritional content is much higher, and the chemicals used to grow non-organic food are not good for your health either. So, in reality, although organically grown food appears to be more expensive, it actually gives you much better value for money as it is full of nutrition; pesticide laden, chemically grown food generally has less nutritional value and is often very depleted in essential vitamins and minerals that are vital for good health.

Eat a variety of fruit and vegetables:

Thirdly, eat a good variety of fresh fruit and vegetables daily. Everyone has heard the '7-a-day rule' now. Try and implement it or even exceed it. Eat as much fresh, raw food as you can. There are lots of vegetables and fruits that you can choose from. Look for things that are inexpensive because they are in 'season'. You can also seek less expensive organic foods by being part of a 'box' scheme or going to a farm shop.

Use good quality oils:

Fat or oil is a vital ingredient in the body because it is one of the main ingredients for building your cells, and your brain consists of about 60 percent fat. As well as buying fresh organic produce, be sure to incorporate beneficial fats into your diet. They are vital for good health. Avoid heavily processed and hydrogenated oils. Do not eat margarine, and don't use rapeseed/canola, or soya oils. Be aware that a lot of pastries and packaged foods have very bad oils in them. The best thing to cook with is coconut oil, butter or butter ghee because they aren't damaged by high temperatures. For salad dressings, use quality extra virgin olive oil, but **don't** cook with it or any other oils or fats not mentioned above.'

Eat fermented food frequently:

Fermented foods are rich in beneficial bacteria which are vital for your health. These bacteria build a good, strong immune system which protects you from harmful disease organisms. They are also responsible for keeping your colon healthy so that you can properly digest your food. They are very important in metabolism and in creating B vitamins in your body. Modern processed foods are totally deficient in beneficial bacteria.

Fermented foods can be found in the cuisines of many cultures as they are a vital dietary need. For instance, in

Eastern European countries you will find sauerkraut and fermented beetroot drinks called kvass. In Asia, you will find kimchi. There are also other fermented drinks such as kombucha and kefir. In addition, there are fermented dairy products such as yogurt. Be sure that the yogurt actually contains live bacterial cultures as some do not.

And of course, beer is also fermented, although the alcohol content makes it less desirable for good health. You can actually ferment any fruit or vegetable; it is an easy process, and highly beneficial. The important thing is not to heat up any of these fermented products as it will kill the bacteria. Have just a little daily - but it doesn't hurt to eat larger amounts too! These are especially helpful if you have been taking antibiotics or other pharmaceutical drugs.

Avoid processed foods

Avoid heavily processed foods, refined flours, and sugar. Not only do they lead to obesity, but also diabetes and other kinds of chronic illness. They are also heavily laden with toxic chemicals and heavy metals which wreak havoc on your body and your immune system. Steer away from very sweet things and avoid caffeine since both of these substances drive the adrenal glands and lead to depletion or adrenal exhaustion.

Avoid drugs

Drugs and alcohol can considerably undermine your health. If you have been using either as a 'resource', then it is time to change if you are able to. The use of drugs can help to temporarily sooth the mental and emotional pain of trauma. However, there comes a point when the benefits are heavily outweighed by the damage done on physical, mental, and emotional levels; they are potentially destructive to relationships, and undermine your ability to have a happy, grounded life.

If you need help to come off them, there are a number of programmes available that will support you, such as Narcotics Anonymous, or Alcoholics Anonymous. If you search the internet you will find other help also. The work of Dr Gabor Maté is well worth researching; he has worked extensively with addiction of all kinds. His conclusion is that it is closely related to trauma. In his book called *"In the Realms of the Hungry Ghosts"*, he shows how addiction to alcohol, narcotics, or other drugs — and also many other addictive behaviours — are a result of trauma.

"Not all traumatised people are addicted but all addicted people are traumatised" – Gabor Maté

Drink plenty of Good Quality Water

Make sure that you get plenty of good quality water every day. Research for a good quality water filter to take out the nasty chemicals that get put into tap water. One recommendation is for Kangen Water that also alkalises the water. You can also buy charcoal to put in a jug of water that takes out the chemicals. Or better still get local spring water if there is some near you. Water from plastic bottles is not advised since the plastic leaches into the water causing health problems and even leading to infertility. You need to aim for about 2 litres of water daily. You can take the water in the form of herb teas. Also, it is a wonderful health support to have lemon juice in water, especially first thing in the morning, to alkalise your body.

Drinks such as tea and coffee are generally considered to not be part of your water intake as they are actually diuretics. Recent research debates that; however, they are still loaded with Caffeine which does acidify your body as well as putting a strain on your adrenaline glands. If you are already quite a 'wired' person and need to rest more, then drink tea and coffee in moderation, or not at all. Some types are better than others.

Your body is made of around 60% of water. When you are dehydrated your immune system is compromised because the white blood cells cannot easily move around. They clump together in your blood which becomes thickened due to the lack of adequate water. In addition, your red blood cells that carry the oxygen begin to collapse and stick together. We need plenty of water to adequately flush toxins from our bodies. Just like having a good supply of water to flush the toilet clean! All of the metabolic processes in our bodies need good clean water, so it is vital for good health.

Take some good quality nutritional supplements

Finally, you may well need some supplements from a good company like BioCare or The Natural Dispensary to boost your health. I would suggest a multi-vitamin and B complex, a high-quality trace mineral supplement such as Ultratrace from BioCare, and either red krill oil or a good quality cod liver oil. Also, a good quality Vitamin C. Don't buy cheap supplements. They are not worth the money that you spend on them.

Ensure good digestion - Eat Quietly and Regularly

Have your meals regularly, and ensure that you can sit quietly to eat so that you are able to digest well. If you are rushing around at the same time as eating, your body will be secreting adrenaline which will shut down the digestion process. You need to be calm so that you can fully digest your food and get the maximum nutrition from it. Try not to eat too late at night, otherwise your liver will be overburdened in the digestion process. For more really good information about nutrition and health, I strongly recommend reading the work of a Naturopathic Doctor called Barbara Wren or finding her on You Tube. Her book called *"Cellular Awakening"* is very in-depth, providing a lot of important information about health.

Employ Simple Health Techniques

Barbara Wren has many ways of healing the body, using simple, naturopathic techniques that are inexpensive, such as using a castor oil pack on the liver. This boosts liver health and good metabolism. Your liver is essential to your well-being and does over 400 different jobs in the body. It is key to your overall health, and really needs taking good care of. For this reason, we should also avoid 'bad' foods, drugs, and alcohol — including pharmaceutical drugs that damage the liver.

Exercise 20

Receiving a Healing Transmission and Visualisation from Myself

My intention for writing this book is to help you to heal. I know that it is entirely possible for you to heal. I have healed myself, and, in my work as a therapist and healer, many, many people have healed. For this reason, I know that whatever you are going through, and no matter how difficult it feels to you, you can also heal. By healing, I mean that your life can be much happier. You can have more ease and freedom, and feel joyful. Your relationships can be better, and your physical health can be much improved.

"You can heal your life"

I would like to take this healing intention further and, in this moment, I am sending you personally, healing energy. If you are ready, would you like to receive it? It is always here for you and you can come back as many times as you like. It is here in infinite abundance. It is not mine to give, it is the life force energy of the Divine or the Infinite Source. I am sitting with it and intending that you should also be open to receiving it.

Make yourself comfortable so that you can receive the healing:

To set the intention on your side, to receive it, make yourself comfortable and perhaps light a candle saying:

'I am open to receiving the life force healing energy of the Divine. I am open to receiving the energy of all that is Sacred'.

Sit quietly and comfortably. Be aware of your breath. Take several deep in-breaths and long out-breaths. Allow yourself to settle into a deeper feeling of comfort. Be aware of your feet, and now your hands. Feel the weight of your body where you are sitting or lying down.

Now imagine that I am here with you. Be aware of a subtle energy field of comfort, love, and support surrounding you. It is calm and protective. You can imagine it in the form of a golden field of loving energy. Every breath that you take brings the healing energy into your body. As you breath it in, it fills your lungs and heart with the warm golden glow of healing energy. It is loving, soothing, and supportive, and strengthens your life force.

Continue to slowly breath in the golden healing energy. Breath it into your blood. Your blood is filled with the warm golden glow, and with each beat of your heart it is being carried around your body, soothing and calming it, loving and caressing it in a gentle healing.

Feel the blood infused with the golden life force, healing energy, being carried around your body to every organ in your body, to your liver, your stomach, your colon, kidneys, and all the other organs, and into your brain. Feel it subtly passing into every cell in your body, infusing you with a golden glow of love and healing.

Now imagine this healing energy expanding from your body out into your energy field. Feel it pulsating with health and love and wellness. It feels really comfortable, warm and protective, and supportive. Feel it now expand to fill the whole room.

It is sure and consistent in its gradual expansion, and it continues to grow around you to build a warm, loving, protective environment that now expands from the room to fill the entire house.

Continue to breath the warm loving golden energy; witness it expanding in an absolute and unstoppable way, out beyond the walls of your house, into the outside world, filling every nook and cranny of the surrounding area to your house.

Continue to breath slowly and deeply; gradually and surely the golden energy expands to the whole of the area, even further, to the whole of the country, and then it continues out into the whole planet. The whole of the earth is surrounded by this warm, golden, protective, loving energy that is flowing outward, embracing everyone with health and healing and love.

Continue to breath the golden energy, knowing that it is infinite and absolute. It is always there. Witness it now extending out into space and surrounding all the planets of the solar system, then filling up the whole galaxy. Going beyond our galaxy to the whole of the Milky Way and even further, to the infinite reaches of the Universe.

Being aware now as you breath the golden energy of love and healing that it is the energy field of the Infinite, the Divine; know that it has always been here and it always will be, and that you are always part of it, no matter what. Know that you can always sit and remember to breath, knowing that you are part of this infinite field of Love.

When you are ready, bring your awareness back to your waking reality, knowing that you are filled with this life force energy that will protect and support you throughout the day.

CHAPTER 7

A Monthly programme with daily exercises

I am wondering how you have been with what I have shared so far? I hope that it has been helpful to you. Here are some easy steps to help you build it into your life.

I have gradually taken you on a step-by-step journey to heal trauma as you have passed through each chapter of this book. The important thing now is whether you can implement this systematically into your life? I know that there will be hurdles, and days when you can do it, and other days when you can't do it — or even whole weeks when you can't.

The important thing is to go at your own pace, and be gentle with yourself.

You don't have to do this in a rigid way. The other important thing is that you need to commit to the process and not let go of it. You need to commit 100% to your healing. It is only when you commit that you get the best results. 80% of success is about showing up. In order to heal, you need to show up for your own life. You need to fully embrace the reality that *'The Past is Over'*. You can now step out of trauma time and into present time.

Once you have committed, it is a matter of systematically working through what I have shown you. You will also find that it is a platform or a guide to enable you to take off and explore other things that can support this core focus of healing.

In order to help you stay on track, I am now writing you a daily schedule, including some suggestions for nourishing food. The schedule runs over 31 days, but you can repeat it as often as you like. In fact, I would suggest that you gradually incorporate it as a way of life. You will find that, as you heal, the exercises you do will change. However, if you continue with a daily mindfulness meditation, it will always be an asset and a beneficial healing experience for you. Healing never stops. We are souls that have an evolutionary path. There are always new challenges and steps along the way to being more and more conscious. A daily practice will help with this.

The other thing, is that I am writing this book for you without knowing exactly what is happening for you. You will have to shape what is written here to suit your own needs. You may be alone and very traumatised, or you may be a busy mum and traumatised, or an executive with a high-pressure job and traumatised. Trauma happens to everyone; it is a human condition. The important thing is, that your daily commitments will affect the way that you can incorporate this schedule. However, take the essence of it, and work with it. Adapt it to your needs. You can also contact me for assistance as part of the healing programmes that I offer at Healing Waters Sanctuary www.julietyelverton.com. I can then help you with your unique difficulties.

The 31 Day Programme

Welcome to the first day of the programme for healing trauma.

Everyone has to start somewhere. Even if you have been unwell for a very long time, it is totally possible to heal the experience, and your life can be entirely different. I am going to help you get back into the driving seat of your life. Read through the instructions and suggestions below, and begin to build awareness of what is helpful and what is not. Creating a journal about this enables you to reflect back to yourself the benefits you are receiving, and the changes that are happening to you as a result of doing this programme.

The first thing to do is to ensure that you are well prepared for the day by eating some healthy and nourishing food. If you have been unwell and stressed for a long time, it may be that you tend to miss breakfast altogether. It is important to have breakfast, so attempt to build something simple and nourishing to support you in this first part of the day.

Here I am going to describe some breakfast choices

BREAKFAST:

1. Porridge:

This is very soothing to the colon and supports your nervous system.

I add a teaspoon of flax seeds into it, which will heal any damage to the colon and help turn off 'dehydration alert' in your body. Barbara Wren talks about this extensively in her book. *'Cellular Awakening'.*

Ingredients:

- ❖ 2 tablespoons of organic oats
- ❖ Half a pint of water
- ❖ A teaspoonful of flax seeds
- ❖ A teaspoonful of goji berries
- ❖ 2 prunes
- ❖ 2 almonds

Optional extra ingredients: You can add in other dried fruits such as raisins, dried or fresh apple, apricots, and even a little chopped ginger is nice. I also chop a very small amount of fresh ginger and turmeric root and add a dash of pepper as these are powerful anti-inflammatory substances.

Alternatives: You can use different kinds of cereal flakes such as barley or rye, or you can use wheat berries (which take longer to cook and need to be pre-soaked).

Time: 15 minutes

Method:

(DO NOT USE A MICROWAVE)

Put water in the saucepan and the teaspoon of flax seeds, also add a teaspoon of goji berries — a superfood — two prunes and two almonds. Add the chopped ginger and turmeric if using and a dash of pepper. Simmer gently for 5 minutes. Now add in two tablespoonfuls of oats and continue simmering. If you prefer a thicker consistency, add in some more oats.

There are different types of oats that you can buy. You can experiment with what you like best. It is best to buy organic oats. However, there are whole oats and there are quick cook oats. Experiment with them. If you are not confident, then start with the quick oats. The whole oats take longer to prepare.

Serve with a milk of your choice, I would suggest either UNHOMOGENISED, RAW cow's milk, goats' milk, almond milk or coconut milk. I do not recommend soy milk, which upsets the hormone levels and is generally genetically modified.

2. Smoothie:

A morning smoothie is very quick to prepare and extremely nutritious. You need a good quality blender if you are going to blend harder vegetables for raw soups or green smoothies, but a normal blender will deal with most soft fruits.

Ingredients:

❖ Banana

❖ Handful of frozen or fresh raspberries

❖ Handful of frozen or fresh blueberries

❖ Half a cup of milk of choice, or water

Method: Put into the blender and whizz together until everything is blended.

Optional extras: You can improve this hugely by adding in a variety of super-foods which will benefit your health. Suggestions to try are: goji berries, raw cacao powder, lucuma powder, maca powder. You can also make it into a green smoothie, which is really good for you, by adding some spirulina, broccoli powder, or mixed greens powder. You can also add in some watercress or spinach leaves. If you make a larger amount you can store some in the fridge for later in the day.

Time: 10 minutes.

3. A pre-soaked cereal breakfast:

This is an easily prepared breakfast, made the night before and kept in the fridge while it soaks overnight. It provides a quick eat-and-go breakfast if you are working. Also, pre-soaking the ingredients makes them more digestible.

Ingredients:

- ❖ 1/2 cup of oats or 6 tablespoons of chia seeds
- ❖ 2 cups of milk of your choice
- ❖ Spices - vanilla, cinnamon or ginger
- ❖ Chopped nuts or seeds
- ❖ Fresh or frozen berries or other dried fruits
- ❖ Optional, a couple of teaspoons of maple syrup

Method:

Mix it all together and put in a bowl in the fridge.

4. Scramble Eggs on Toast:

Ingredients:

- ❖ 2 slices of organic wholemeal bread (or other healthy bread of your choice)
- ❖ 2 FREE RANGE eggs, preferably organic
- ❖ about a tablespoon of butter or ghee
- ❖ salt and pepper to taste

Method:

Break the eggs into a bowl and whisk together with a fork or mixer until you have totally merged yolks with the whites.

Put the butter in a small saucepan on a very low heat until it is melted. Do not allow it to overheat.

Put your toast on to cook and make sure that it is going to automatically pop up so that it does not distract you from doing the eggs.

Now add in your eggs, keeping the heat low. Stir with a wooden spoon and you will see that the eggs gradually begin to thicken. If you cook too fast, they will separate into having a watery substance and hard egg parts. This is still okay to eat, but not as nice as the creamy eggs which you will get from slow cooking.

Butter your toast and serve the eggs on it.

Optional extras: You can add such things as tomatoes, peppers, cheese, or smoked salmon to your eggs.

Time: 20 minutes.

Other breakfast choices:

- Eggs in other forms - boiled, poached, fried
- Avocado on toast
- Beans on toast
- Fruit salad
- Left-overs from the night before!

DRINKS WITH BREAKFAST:

Steer away from Caffeine-laden drinks such as tea, and especially coffee or hot chocolate laden with sugar. Choose a herb tea, preferably like chamomile for relaxation or peppermint, fennel or ginger for your digestion. And, of course, a glass of water with lemon juice in is very good. It is best not to drink at the same time as eating as it impairs digestion. Half an hour before or after food is best.

LUNCHES:

Eating a light to medium lunch every day is very beneficial for your health. Here are some suggestions. You can build on the basic format.

- Salad:
- Soup:
- Steamed Vegetables with Rice or other grains.

How to make a Salad:

There are many different approaches to salad-making, and lots of possible ingredients. The best ingredients are those that are fresh and green, preferably organic, and preferably picked from your own garden or, if not, from a farm shop or organic community garden.

Typical ingredients are parsley, rocket, small spinach leaves, lettuce leaves of various types. You can also add wild leaves that are very good for your health like dandelion or sorrel, and flowers such as daisies, nasturtiums, and borage — each of which have health giving properties.

Alongside the leaves you add, are ingredients like grated or chopped carrots, beetroot, spring onions, peppers, celery, radish, or shredded cabbage — red or white. You can also add sunflower, pumpkin, or sesame seeds to create more protein and an interesting texture. Chopped up fruit or steamed green beans can also be included, as can feta cheese, blue cheese, or tuna. The combinations are endless. The important thing is to just make as much as you would like to eat in one sitting. It doesn't stay fresh for long.

Salad dressings:

There are lots of recipes for salad dressings, but the basis of them is oil and vinegar, or lemon juice. I choose a really good quality extra virgin, cold pressed olive oil, or maybe walnut oil. Then I mix it with a slightly smaller amount of either freshly pressed lemon juice or apple cider vinegar. These are two very life-giving ingredients. I add in some herbs or maybe half a teaspoonful of honey, some French mustard, and some chopped garlic or garlic powder, and mix or shake well. Alternatively, you can just pour a little olive oil and lemon juice onto your salad.

Other things to serve with your salad:

The best ingredient to have with your salad is avocado, which is the perfect food for good health. You can also have sardines, or beans of some kind, or hard-boiled eggs, or maybe some smoked fish or salmon, or even a piece of quiche.

How to make a soup:

Soups are really quick and simple. My favourite method is simple. You can use the butternut soup recipe below and substitute another root vegetable, or other squash or courgette for different flavors.

Soups can also be blended or unblended pieces of vegetables. You can also add in red or other lentils that are quick to cook, and flavour with a variety of herbs or some Indian spices.

Ingredients for a butternut soup.

- ❖ Half a butternut squash
- ❖ 1 onion
- ❖ clove of garlic and piece of ginger
- ❖ Half a teaspoonful of marjoram
- ❖ Heaped teaspoonful of vegetable bouillon, such as Marigold
- ❖ Salt and pepper to season
- ❖ 1 – 2 pints of water, or you can make it half milk

Method:

Choose your vegetable and cut into small pieces, for instance, butternut squash. Also chop one onion and some garlic and or ginger. Sautee everything gently using a little coconut oil. When they start to stick, add in the water. Allow to simmer for about 10 minutes. Add in some herbs such as thyme, parsley, oregano, marjoram; some vegetable bouillon, salt and pepper. If using milk, add it in at the end.

When the vegetables are cooked, turn off the heat and blend with a hand-held soup blender. They are very cheap to buy, and much easier than pouring hot soup into a glass blender.

If you are using other vegetables, even leafy greens such as spinach, then you use the same method. A lovely, nourishing soup is potato and nettle; for this, use two potatoes and a large, gloved handful of freshly picked and rinsed nettle tops. Take the first 4 leaves when picking the nettles as the lower leaves and stalk can be tough. Add the nettles to the soup as the last thing before blending.

If you make an unblended soup, you can include a mixture of vegetables. Sauté them, then add in your water and also add in half a cup of red lentils. In this case ensure that you have enough liquid as the lentils cook, so that they don't stick. You can flavour this with herbs such as sage, mint, rosemary, parsley; or make a dahl-style soup with spices such as paprika, cumin, coriander, turmeric, ginger. Add the spices at the sautéing stage.

Other lunch suggestions:

* Egg dishes of all kinds
* A sandwich
* Quiche

- Cheese and tomato on toast
- Mushrooms on toast
- Noodles and stir fry veg.
- Vegetable dahl

EVENING MEALS:

It is best not to eat too late into the evening. Here are some basic suggestions for easy to prepare meals.

1. Baked Potatoes and Salad

Ingredients:

❖ Salad, made as already described above.

❖ 1 or 2 medium to large potatoes; well washed with any eye's or 'black bits' taken out. If you get already cleaned potatoes this is unlikely to be a problem.

Method:

Put the washed potatoes directly on the middle shelf of the oven. DO NOT MICROWAVE THEM. Cook for about an hour or 45 minutes at a medium heat. Gas mark 6 or 7 or Electric around 250 degrees. You can test if they are cooked by sticking a fork into them. If they are easy to pierce then they are ready. Let the skins get a little crispy before taking them out.

2. Steamed Vegetables and Rice:

Ingredients.

❖ Basmati, long grain rice, or brown rice — long grain preferably. Brown rice takes longer to cook and needs slightly more water. You need approximately half to a whole cup of dried rice, depending on your appetite. You can store it and use it again next day if you have made too much.

❖ Vegetables. Typical choice could be, 1 carrot, 1 piece of calabrese broccoli, 2 pieces of butternut squash. Portion of green beans, half a parsnip. Choose vegetables that you like.

Method:

1. Rice. Put roughly twice as much water as rice into the saucepan. If it is white rice then slightly less water. Then bring gently to the boil. If white rice, then boil for a few minutes with the lid on, but not completely on as it may boil over. Then turn it off and leave it to stand fully covered. It will go on cooking in its own heat. With brown rice you do the same but you continue to simmer it for about 20 to 30 minutes, or until all the water is gone. You can then taste if the rice is cooked. Do not stir it around when cooking as this makes it sticky. If the water is gone and it is still not cooked then add a small amount of extra water in to it.

2. Steaming the vegetables. Chop them into equal sized pieces and place in a steamer. Add in the root vegetables first and cook for a couple of minutes before adding the leafy vegetables which take less time to cook. Place the steamer on a saucepan of hot water and steam for about 5

– 7 minutes. Even less time is okay. Just steam until they are at the right consistency for you. Less cooked is healthier.

Serve with olive oil and tamari or soy sauce.

3. Lightly steamed fish and Sautéed Vegetables:

Ingredients:

- ❖ Fish of your choice. It is probably easiest to get a fish fillet of some kind that does not involve preparing the fish

- ❖ A choice of vegetables: such as carrots, onions, peppers, courgettes, green beans, squash

- ❖ Ginger root and Garlic clove chopped

- ❖ Any other vegetables that you like

- ❖ Butter and or coconut oil for cooking

- ❖ Herbs and salt and pepper

Method:

Put the fish in some tin foil; add a little butter, some herbs such as parsley, salt and pepper and a slice of lemon. Place the seasoned, foil-wrapped fish in the steamer. This will only take about 5 minutes to steam. Alternatively, you can put the fish into a frying pan with a little bit of butter and other ingredients, put a lid on, and cook gently for about 5 minutes.

Sautéed Vegetables. Cut the vegetables into equal sizes. Place a knob of coconut oil, or some butter, into the pan.

Allow it to melt on a gentle heat. Add in the onion, garlic, and ginger. Sautee for a minute on a gentle heat. Now add the other vegetables, and cook on a gentle heat with the lid on. Add in any leafy vegetables last. Cook for around 5 minutes on a low heat. You will need to stir it several times. If it starts to stick, add in about a tablespoonful of water.

4. Pasta and Sauce.

Ingredients:

- ❖ Pasta of choice, preferably whole meal. It can be any of the shaped pastas. Or you can use gluten free pasta if you have a gluten difficulty.
- ❖ A tablespoon of olive oil.

Ingredients for the sauce.

- ❖ 1 onion
- ❖ 1 clove of garlic
- ❖ Several fresh tomatoes or a tin of tomatoes
- ❖ Half a green pepper
- ❖ Half a courgette
- ❖ Then you can choose, either several anchovies from a tin, or half a tin of sweet corn, or some Quorn pieces, you can buy them frozen. A handful of black or green olives. A handful of capers. Or anything that appeals to you to add into the basic sauce.
- ❖ Herbs such as marjoram, thyme, oregano, basil, salt and pepper.
- ❖ Butter to cook. Or olive oil if you cook it on a low heat.

Method:

Pasta.

Put a large-sized pan of water on to boil. Have about 4 pints of water for 8 oz. of pasta. You will need about 4ozs of pasta for one person, depending on appetite, which would then need 2 pints of water. Add in the olive oil to prevent the pasta sticking. When the water is boiling, add the pasta and stir gently to separate. If you are using spaghetti, feed it in down one side of the pan until it is all submerged. Boil with the lid off for about 10 minutes. You can taste when it is cooked properly. If it is overcooked it will be sticky; if under cooked, a little hard. When done, drain it through a sieve (if it is sticky you can pour some more water over it, hot or cold, letting it drain through).

The Sauce.

Add the chopped onion and garlic to the olive oil or butter in the bottom of the pan. Let it sauté gently for a couple of minutes on a low heat. Then add the peppers and courgette. Now add the tomatoes and the other ingredients of choice. Cook gently for about 10 minutes on a low heat.

5. Stir fry Vegetables and Rice.

Ingredients:

- ❖ Rice, either basmati or brown rice
- ❖ Selection of vegetables of choice. Suggestions are onion, garlic, ginger, carrots, peppers, broccoli, courgette, leafy greens, baby sweet corn, green beans, mange tout peas.

- ❖ Coconut oil
- ❖ Tamari
- ❖ salt and pepper

Method:

Rice preparation. Please do the same as described previously.

Stir fry: Chop the vegetables into thin strips, where applicable, and the onion into small pieces. Chop the ginger and garlic.

When the rice is almost done, place the coconut oil in a large, shallow pan or wok. When hot, add the vegetables in quick succession, stirring all the time. Put the onion, garlic, ginger, and carrots in first. Add in the leafy greens and mange tout peas for the last 30 seconds. Should the pan get too hot, add in a tablespoon full of water. The idea is to cook the vegetables just up to the point of being a little crunchy. When cooked, serve on top of the rice and season with tamari, salt and pepper if you wish.

These recipes are the basis for lots of variations. You can gradually add more things. There are many foods that are quick, easy, and nutritious. If you have a computer and access to the internet, you can find many things on YouTube; simply search for your favourite styles of cooking or food types.

CHAPTER 8

Blocks to Healing

If you are 100% committed, and you take the focussed time to follow the process, there is no doubt that you will heal. However, there are possible blocks to this happening. Some of these blocks may arise more from your mind than an actual physical reason why you cannot get better. Others may be a result of your living circumstances; even so, you can change them when you approach them with conscious intention.

Limiting Beliefs:

The nature of trauma is that it creates a limiting belief around the aspects of your life which were affected by the traumatising event. You may feel that, no matter how much you try, you will never get well. Or that you are always abandoned, or that you will never find love in your life. The effect of trauma on your nervous system means that, when you are triggered, the same neurons (neurons are cells in the brain that send information) are going to fire over and over, leading to the same thought processes, which then affect your emotions and your belief in the possibility of change. This, in itself, is a symptom of the trauma. With conscious awareness, you can heal this symptom and heal your trauma.

Limiting Circumstances:

Another block to healing, is if you are still in a situation that is causing you trauma. You may be living in an abusive relationship, or in a family with members suffering from addiction. Or you could be suffering chronically ill heath, or looking after another individual with ill health. Perhaps you are in a situation of poverty and you feel ground down by your life? All these circumstantial situations can make it feel like it is too difficult to heal.

The other thing is if you are with someone who is continually controlling you, and undermining your intentions towards change or good health. Similarly, you may feel blocked if you are in a co-dependent relationship wherein you are kept feeling helpless. They may make you feel like you would never cope if you left them to live on your own. They could be doing things that make you feel like you are crazy or stupid.

These are all very difficult situations to be in, and they may give you a distorted perception of yourself. You may find it hard to know who you really are, or what you can really achieve. Despite these issues, there is no doubt that you can change, and that you can get better. It may take more effort but you can still recover. It is important to know that you — like every other human being — have the same potential to heal. Human beings are remarkable in how much they can change.

In order to create the right conditions for change, it is firstly necessary to create an awareness of what might be blocking you. Take time to create a list of possible obstacles. Learn to identify your limiting beliefs about healing. Write also, about the limiting circumstances that you are in, and notice what it is that keeps you locked into that situation. Notice your inner voice that tells you that you will never be well. Give the voice a name and learn to tell that voice to 'be quiet, you don't know everything'.

When you have your list of obstacles, write another list of possible solutions to those obstacles. It doesn't matter how unlikely it feels, just allow your imagination to run with ideas to overcome the obstacles. Write down everything that comes to mind, and out of that will come a path forward to a different approach to your life.

When you have your list of solutions, imagine the kind of person that you would need to be in order to implement those solutions. What are the qualities that you would need to have to bring some change in your life? Describe the character, the personality and the qualities of that person who is able to do that. Now set your intention to move towards embracing those qualities in yourself. You can do this. We can change ourselves on all levels.

CHAPTER 9

Starting your Trauma Resolution Programme

Welcome to the healing trauma programme. Firstly, know that even if you have been unwell for a long time, it is totally possible to heal this experience, and your life can be entirely different. I am going to help you get back into the driving seat of your life. The important thing is to slowly build your resources and implement, day-by-day, healthy eating and sleeping patterns.

With the exercises, it is important not to skip ahead, but to slowly build yourself up — as previously described. Do the exercises at your own pace, according to your levels of activation. You are learning to self-regulate your nervous system; the chart and diary will help you get a feel for how you are coping, and where you are at with it. It may happen that you will have 'healing experiences or crisis' coming up. If this is the case. Go slower in the exercises or return to an earlier one until things begin to settle.

If you still get overwhelmed, I suggest you seek out some professional help if need be. My contact details are at the end of the book, or go to either of my websites www.julietyelverton.com or www.healing-waters.co.uk for therapies.

Day 1

Exercise 1: Planning or Visioning Your Resources (Pg 68)

After you have had a healthy breakfast, take your supplements. Or if instructed to take them on an empty stomach, then follow the advice on the package. You can choose some appropriate supplements from the list at the end of Chapter 5.

Today, we are going to start with the resourcing exercise *'Planning or Visioning Your Resources'*. You will need a large piece of paper and some coloured pens or crayons. Refer back to Chapter 4, Exercise 1 page 68.

When you have finished this, decide what you would like to do today to resource yourself. Choose something from the Resource Plan that you have made.

Remember to take the time to make a healthy lunch for yourself, and plan something for the afternoon. You may already have something that you have to do; if so, make sure that there is enough time built into the day for yourself.

Ensure that you have a healthy dinner no later than 7pm.

Day 2

Resources Review (pg 67)

Refer again to Chapter 4 page 67 if you need to.

After a healthy breakfast, take your supplements.

Take out the resource plan you created yesterday. Create a quiet space for yourself and sit down with it. See if there is anything that you would like to add. Now see if you can make a plan on how to resource yourself, each day, for the rest of the week. Which things on your 'resources plan' are the easiest to implement? You will need a diary; if you don't have one, write down the days of the week on a piece of paper, with space for notes for each day. Next, write down a resourcing activity for each day of this week.

Now refer to your activation chart. Note how you are feeling; write it down on the chart. Alternatively, enter into your diary how you felt about planning a resource for yourself.

Eat a healthy lunch and do something nice for yourself in the afternoon.

Eat a healthy dinner before 7pm.

Day 3

Exercise 2: Somatic Experiencing (pg 89)

After a healthy breakfast, take your supplements.

Now take the time to create a comfortable space for yourself. Refer to the Somatic Experiencing section in Chapter 4 page 89 and follow the instructions.

When you are finished, write the session up in your diary. Describe how you felt at the beginning of the session, and how you felt at the end of it. Also mark up on your activation how you feel now.

Now plan what you are going to do in the afternoon or evening to resource yourself.

Take time for a healthy lunch today. Eat in an unhurried way, quietly, without disturbances.

After lunch, at the time that you have organised for yourself, follow through on your resource activity.

Day 4

Exercise 3: Visualising a Place Where You Feel Good
(pg 97)

Take the time to make yourself a nourishing breakfast, and eat it slowly without disturbance. After breakfast, take your supplements.

This morning, please refer to Chapter 4, Exercise 3 page 97 for the 'Visualisation in a Place Where You Feel Good' exercise. Please make yourself comfortable and set the intention for a healing visualisation. Read through the exercise, then settle yourself in comfortably.

After you have finished, please describe the place you visualised, and how you felt when doing the exercise. Now mark on your activation chart how activated you are. Notice the difference from when you started the exercise.

Now think about what your resource activity is for later in the day. Do you need to do any preparation for it?

Around midday, make your lunch and then eat it in a comfortable way. Turn off your phone, put it out of sight and make sure you won't be disturbed so you can relax whilst eating. After lunch, when you are ready, make the time to do your resourcing. What have you got that is special for yourself today?

Have a healthy evening meal no later than 7pm

Create a small ritual around going to bed that supports you having a peaceful and comfortable night's sleep. Refer to the section on Sleep in Chapter 3 page 85. Aim to go to bed around 10pm, but certainly before midnight.

Day 5

Exercise 2: Somatic Experiencing (Repeat)

Have a leisurely healthy breakfast. After breakfast, take your supplements.

This morning, take the time to reflect on how the week has been since you began this process from day one, and write about it in your diary. Then, when you are ready, create a comfortable space to do the Somatic Experiencing exercise again at the start of Chapter 4. When you have finished, note in your diary if anything was different from when you did it the day before yesterday. Also note how the exercise was for you. Mark on your activation chart how activated you are.

When you have done this, get out your resource plan and refresh your mind as to what resources you have available to you; see if there is anything else that you want to add to it. Choose what you will do later in the day.

Around midday, make yourself a healthy lunch and eat it in a quiet, unhurried manner. Notice the flavours of the food; take time to digest fully.

After lunch, when you are ready, do your resourcing. As you do the resourcing, notice how it feels in your body. What is happening for you as you do the things that you have planned? For instance, if it involves physical exercise, notice how it feels whilst you're doing it. What are the bodily sensations?

Have a nourishing meal around 7pm. You may need to prepare for it around 6pm. Whilst eating, notice again the flavours of the food and the sensation of eating.

Before bed, prepare your routine for a good night's sleep. Tonight, take a moment to set the intention for remembering your dreams.

Day 6:

Make yourself a healthy breakfast and eat in an unhurried manner. After breakfast, take your supplements.

When you are ready, get out your diary and note down any dream that you recall, or any 'feeling tone' from your dream that you remember; that is, a sense of what the dream was, or if there was something familiar about it.

Create a comfortable space and do the somatic experiencing exercise in Chapter 4 again. After the exercise, write down what it was like, and make a note of activation levels on your chart.

Plan what you are going to do today for resourcing. Did you create a list of people that you would like to build into your network of connections? Or is there a group that you want to reach out and join?

Around midday, prepare your lunch and eat in an unhurried way, making sure that there are no disturbances. Be aware of how the food tastes and what the feelings are in your body as you eat.

After lunch, or sometime later in the day, do your resource activity. Again, notice the body sensations of what you are doing.

Prepare your evening meal around 6pm. As you are doing the preparation, be aware of the sensations of the movements that you are making. Be aware also of your activation levels.

Eat in an unhurried manner.

Around 10pm, prepare for bed with a routine to ensure comfort. Do you need to add anything to ensure a better sleep? Set an intention to have happy, positive dreams, and to be able to remember them. If you have been disturbed by bad dreams, write a note reminding yourself that you are entirely safe, and anything dreamt is unreal, or a memory. Place it where you will see if you wake in the night.

Day 7

Exercise 3: Visualising a Place where you feel good (repeat)

Chapter 4,

Start the day today with some lemon juice in warm water — before you have your normal drink of the day.

Eat a healthy breakfast. Notice how you are feeling physically as you prepare your breakfast. Eat in a slow, unhurried fashion — savouring the food — and notice your body sensations as you eat. After breakfast, take your supplements.

When you are ready, get out your diary and write down any dreams you had the night before.

Create a comfortable place for yourself in preparation for doing the 'Visualising a Place Where You Feel Good' exercise from Chapter 4 again.

When you have finished, write in your diary what it was like and how it was different from last time, then mark your level of activation on your chart. Plan your resources for the day. Ensure that it involves movement in some way.

Around midday, prepare your lunch. As you do the preparation, notice the colours and the textures of the ingredients you are using, and be aware of the smells of the cooking. As you eat your lunch in an unhurried way, notice the flavours and the sensation of eating.

After lunch, anticipate what pleasurable activity you are going to do today and imagine yourself doing that activity.

Prepare your evening meal around 6pm, again being aware of the sensory experience of the preparation, noting colour, texture, and smells. When eating in an unhurried fashion, be aware of flavours and sensations.

Around 10pm, prepare your bedtime ritual. Set an intention for a good night's sleep and with positive, happy dreams that you will remember.

Day 8

Exercise 4: Boundaries (pg 101)

Start your day with some lemon juice in hot water, then make yourself a healthy breakfast, eaten in quietness. Be aware of the whole process of eating in a calm manner with no distractions, taking time to relish and enjoy your food, knowing that it is nourishing your body and preparing you for the day.

This morning, you are going move on in the process of healing but, firstly, assess how you are doing at this stage. Is everything doable for you, and do you feel stable with what we have done so far? Do you need to actually go back to the beginning and redo the exercises from last week? It really is okay to go at your own pace; small steps actually give bigger, more permanent improvements to your nervous system. If you have checked in, and you feel okay to go to the next stage, then let us continue.

When you are ready, get out your diary and just note if you have had any dreams that are important for you. When done, we start the Boundary Exercise which is on page 101. You will need coloured pens and paper.

When you have finished, note how it was for you in your diary; did anything important come up when doing the exercise? Also note your activation level on the chart.

When completed, plan your resourcing activity for the day,

At around midday, prepare your lunch — being mindful of the process. Have an awareness of the colours, textures, and smells of the food. Be in the present moment with the experience.

You may today want to give thanks for your lunch, or say grace. You can say something like:

'Blessings on the food' or *'I give thanks for this food'* or — one that I like — is to thank everyone and everything who has been involved in the process of creating the food. *'Thank you to the sun, the rain, the earth, and the earthworms; also to the people who grew this food. Thank you to the harvesters and packers. And, above all, thank you to the Divine Essence that brought this food to me.'*

Or if you have Buddhist leanings, here is another prayer:

'I give thanks to the three Precious Jewels. The precious Buddha, the precious Dharma, and the precious Sangha. Please bless this food so that it may nourish my body with my mind free from attachment and desire, and that I may work for the good of all sentient beings. Om Mane Padme Hum.'

You may find that saying grace makes you feel more peaceful and receptive to the food. Enjoy it, savouring the flavours and textures.

After lunch, when you are ready, enjoy something that will resource you.

Have your evening meal around 7pm; again, preparation would start around 6pm. Allow yourself to be really centred and mindful of the preparation, and present to the experience of it.

Eat it quietly and reflectively.

Prepare for bed around 10pm, doing anything that you need to do for a good night's sleep. Before going to sleep, give thanks for your day.

Day 9

Exercise 5: Physically Implementing Your Circles

See Chapter 4 Page 105

Start your day with a glass of lemon water. Then enjoy a peaceful breakfast, taking your supplements afterwards.

After breakfast, get out your diary and write down any dreams or important realisations that have come to you, or how you feel that you are proceeding with your healing process.

Today, we are going to do another boundary exercise; the one of physically creating the boundaries on the floor as described in page 101. When you have completed the exercise, write in your diary what came up for you; also note your activation levels.

Next, plan what you are going to do for resourcing. Have you now found a group or activity where you can enjoy some creative time and build social contacts? You might want to reconsider this if it hasn't happened yet.

Around midday, prepare your lunch in a mindful way, remembering to feel your feet on the ground as you are preparing it, and being aware of the movement of your limbs. Be conscious of the feel of the cooking implements, textures, sensations, and temperature.

When prepared, say grace if you like, or at the least have a moment's silence to acknowledge that you are about to nourish your body.

After lunch, or sometime in the rest of the day, do your resourcing activity — even if it is just a short walk. You are doing really well; give yourself a big pat on the back for your dedication to your healing process.

Around 6pm, begin preparing for your evening meal, again being mindful of the process. As at lunch time, notice the feel, the density, the textures, and temperature of the equipment you are using.

Eat in a peaceful fashion, and, afterwards, enjoy your evening. If you find your mind drifting into any unpleasant or negative things, tell yourself that the past is over and done with and that you are now safe in the present moment.

Around 10pm, prepare for bed with whatever ritual you enjoy to create comfort. Before going to sleep, affirm your intention for a good night's sleep, and for a healed body and mind.

DAY 10

Exercise 6: Saying 'NO' (pg 110)

Begin your day with a glass of water and lemon juice, and then make yourself an enjoyable breakfast when you are ready. After breakfast, take your supplements.

Now get out your diary and write down any significant dreams, or how you are feeling today.

This morning we are going to do the *'Saying No'* exercise. You may want to practice this over the next two days, we repeat the same thing tomorrow.

Ensure that you are well resourced when you start this exercise, being aware somatically of the place of comfort and well-being in your body.

After the exercise, write in your diary how the exercise was for you, and if it brought up any issues or difficult feelings. Also note on your activation chart how you are feeling.

When this is completed, plan your resourcing activity for the day.

Now prepare your lunch with full awareness. If you have any distractions as a result of doing the exercise, gently bring yourself back into noticing the sensations of the food preparation. When lunch is ready, say 'grace' if you feel moved to, and eat with a gentle awareness of the food nourishing your body.

After lunch, and whenever you are ready, enjoy your activity of the day.

Make your evening meal around 6pm, again with full awareness of the physical sensations of the food preparation, savouring smells and colours. Prepare yourself with a pleasant anticipation of what you going to eat tonight.

Eat slowly and consciously, taking time to properly chew each mouthful, knowing that it is fully nourishing your body.

Around 10pm, prepare for bed, doing whatever you need to do to ensure a really good night's sleep. Set the intention upon going to sleep that your boundaries are strong around you, and that you are entirely safe and well in the present moment.

DAY 11

Exercise 6: Saying 'NO' (repeat)

Welcome to another day full of hope and promise of total wellness! Enjoy your lemon and water, knowing that it is cleansing and preparing your body for good health. Make yourself a nourishing breakfast and eat slowly with a pleasant anticipation of the day ahead of you.

After breakfast, get out your diary and write down any dreams that you may have had, and also how you are feeling this morning after the earlier exercise of saying 'NO'.

This morning, you are going to repeat this exercise so that you fully embody it. It is your right to say 'NO' to anything that threatens to transgress the boundaries that you have created. They are your boundaries, and it is your territory and your life, and you are empowered to say 'NO' to whatever is not serving you or helping you be well. Complete the exercise again with full consciousness of your sovereign right to say 'NO'; ensure that your 'NO' is said with full strength and authority. When you are fully satisfied with the strength of your 'NO', you can finish the exercise.

Now write in your diary how that experience was for you, and how you would like to implement it in your life. Write about the situations that come up for you in the present part of your life where you are going to ensure that you say 'NO' when necessary. After this, mark your activation chart.

Now plan your relaxing, resourcing activity for the day. See if you are creating a balance in the activities that you are doing, and that you are getting a chance to either socialise or to have peace, whichever is the most important for you.

With anticipation of a pleasant, peaceful lunch, make the preparations, being fully present to this part of lunch. It is as if you are being nourished by the sight, touch, and smell of the food before you have even eaten it.

When it is ready, sit and take a pause, with an intention of being well nourished; say 'grace' if you like, and enjoy your meal.

After lunch, or when you are ready, do whatever you have planned for the day.

At around 6pm, make your evening meal, again being present to the process of food preparation and engaging with the sensations of it. Ensure you are preparing foods which are both nourishing and enjoyable to you.

Eat your meal with a restful state of mind, and quiet enjoyment.

Have a peaceful, non-stimulating evening, and around 10pm, prepare for bed. Give some thanks for the day, and for what you have achieved in setting some clear boundaries in your life. Before going to sleep, set your intention for a restful, healing sleep.

DAY 12

Chapter 4 - Exercise 7: Physical Gesture of STOP (pg 116)

Good morning! Enjoy a glass of good water and lemon juice, you may have it cold or slightly warm. Prepare and enjoy a nourishing breakfast. After breakfast, remember to take your supplements.

When you are ready, get out your diary and write any dreams or anything that has come up for you around saying 'NO'. Also note your overall state of wellbeing.

Today, we are going to start the 'PUSHING ARMS' exercise. We will again do this over 2 days, so that the frozen trauma energies have the opportunity to clear. Read through the exercise again.

When you are ready and have set up the space to do this, proceed with the exercise, ensuring that you go through it slowly.

After the exercise, get out your diary and write down how the exercise was and what came up for you. Now mark your level of activation on the chart.

Plan your resourcing activity for the day, reviewing it and seeing if you can add anything to the things that you do. Are there any more resources that would support you?

When you are ready, around midday, prepare lunch; notice if you are now able to be in the present moment when you are doing this, and whether you are focussing your awareness on the sensations of the food preparation. If you are not, then gently bring yourself into that awareness.

Have the same consideration when eating your lunch. *'Am I present to the full experience of nourishing and supporting my body?'* Eat with an intention to nourish and heal yourself.

After lunch, whenever you choose, engage in your resourcing activity. When you do your resourcing, again do it with the conscious awareness that you are doing something to fully support your healing.

For the evening meal, around 6pm, again do your food preparation in a way that supports you on every level. Eat slowly, with full conscious awareness of how the food is nourishing you — mind, body, and soul — and that you are healing on every level.

Have a quiet, reflective evening. Do not work or engage in anything stimulating or stressful.

Prepare for bed around 10pm, with an intention for a quiet, restful night.

DAY 13

Exercise 8: Pushing Arms (pg 122)

Start your day with lemon juice and water, and then prepare breakfast — eating it in a peaceful manner. Take your supplements after breakfast.

When you get your diary out, reflect on any dreams you had, and how are you feeling after doing the exercise yesterday. Did it bring anything up for you? This morning, you are going to repeat it and see how this feels. Do it slowly, and track your sensations. Give space and time for the process to complete.

When you have completed the exercise, write in your diary if anything else comes up, then make a note on your activation chart. Now plan your resourcing activity for the day.

Around midday, when this is all completed, begin your meal preparation. Make this an enjoyable process; know that you are fully competent at nourishing your body. Eat with satisfaction.

Sometime during the afternoon, do your resourcing activity; again, be aware of how it helps your body feel relaxed and in the present moment.

Prepare your evening meal around 6pm, and do it with full consciousness, nourishing your body on all levels with the sensation of the food preparation. Eat peacefully, and savour the food.

Have a quiet, non-stimulating evening, perhaps doing a simple craft activity such as knitting, sewing, model-making, a jigsaw, or other relaxing craftwork. Something that occupies your hands.

Around 10pm, prepare for a good night's sleep. Before going to sleep, set your intention to be totally healed.

DAY 14

Refer to Chapter 4 - Exercises 7-9 Pushing Legs (pg 116)

This morning, have some lemon juice and water prior to a nourishing breakfast, followed by your supplements. You should be slowly building this to be an automatic ritual, your good start to the day, regardless of what follows.

After breakfast, write in your diary how you feel after the work of yesterday with pushing arms, and if you had any significant dreams.

The exercise this morning is the same, but now you are going to push with your legs to clear frozen trauma energies. Read through the exercise again, if you need to. Do the exercise slowly to enable energies to clear.

When you have completed this, write in your diary if it brought up any memories, and how you feel afterwards. Mark on your activation chart how you are feeling now.

Now plan your resourcing for today. Review if you are getting enough exercise in the fresh air. You need to be getting out at least once a day.

Around midday, make yourself a nourishing lunch. Remember - by taking in the sensory awareness of how things look, taste, and smell - you are healing your nervous system. Build this awareness into everything that you do. Eat your lunch in a slow manner so that you digest well.

After lunch, or whenever you have planned it, do your resourcing activity.

Around 6pm, prepare your evening meal. Reflect again on the sensations of doing this, and have an anticipation of being nourished by the food.

Have a restful evening and, around 10pm, prepare your bedtime ritual to ensure a calm, restful sleep.

DAY 15

Exercise 9: Pushing Legs (repeat)

Good morning. Start your day with lemon juice and water, so that your body begins with a gentle detox. As you cleared the energies yesterday, you need to assist them being excreted from your body in this way. Now have a good breakfast followed by your supplements.

After breakfast, write in your diary if anything came up as a result of your work yesterday, or if you had any significant dreams.

Today, you are going to repeat the 'Pushing Legs' exercise. When you have done this, note how it was for you in your diary and on your activation chart.

Plan your resources for the day.

After this, remember to bring your full awareness to the preparation and consumption of both your lunch and evening meal; make sure they are nutritious, and include a good amount of fresh fruit and vegetables.

Make your evening a restful and non-stimulating time, and your bedtime ritual supportive for a good night's sleep.

DAY 16

Exercise 10: Preparing to Run or Fight (pg 128)

Proceed with your day in the manner described from Days 1 – 15, with diligent attention given to good nutrition and resourcing yourself each day. Also continue to write up your ongoing experience of the exercises, and noting on your activation charts after the exercises.

If you need support for any of this, read the prior days again, but follow the exercise schedule that I will continue to write for you.

In the exercise today, we are going to continue with releasing frozen trauma energies from your body.

DAY 17

Exercise 11: Mindfulness Meditation - Tracking the Way That You Embody Emotions. (Pg130)

Read through the description of mindfulness meditation and do the practice for this morning. If you become overly activated then bring in your dual awareness skills.

Remember to track your activation levels, and keep a record of what has come up for you in your diary.

DAY 18

Exercise 11: Mindfulness Meditation - Tracking the Way That You Embody Emotions (repeat Day 17)

DAY 19

Exercise 12: Mindfulness Meditation – Allowing your body to express movement (pg 134)

This is a follow on from the first step of the mindfulness meditation and it helps to release the frozen trauma energies from your body. Remember to note your activation and to write it up in your diary.

DAY 20

Exercise 12: Mindfulness Meditation - Allowing Your Body to Express Movement (repeat of yesterday).

DAY 21

Exercise 13: Releasing Higher Levels of Activation (pg 140)

Today, we are going to develop the practice releasing higher levels of activation by going deeper into your own history and experiences and using the resources and techniques you have been already using.

DAY 22

Exercise 14: Practicing Dual Awareness (pg 142)

Today, we are going to develop the practice of Dual Awareness. Read through the description of it before starting. Go through the practice and notice if this helps at all with your activation levels. Throughout the day — if you find yourself triggered — bring in this dual awareness alongside your somatic awareness of well-being.

DAY 23

Re-read Chapter 5: Working with the emotions.

Today, you can begin to work with the emotions that have come up for you. Notice which of the sections described resonate with you, and do the work on that emotion — either within a mindfulness meditation or using EFT.

DAY 24

Chapter 6, Exercise 17: Writing a Release Letter

Read through the exercise on page 195. Remember to give yourself plenty of time and space. You can choose to redo the exercise for different people.

DAY 25

Exercise 18: Creating a ritual with your letter

Read through the exercise on page 197. Remember to give yourself plenty of time and space. You can choose to redo the exercise for different people.

DAY 26

Exercise 19: Practicing Gratitude

Read through the exercise on page 199 first and then practice it. You can bring this practice into your awareness on a daily basis.

DAY 27

Exercise 20: Receiving a Healing Transmission and Visualisation from Myself.

Read through the description of this healing first on page 221. You could read it and record it and then sit with it as you listen to your recording.

DAY 28

Understanding Your Blocks

Re-read Chapter 8 – Blocks to Healing

Make a list of any blocks to your healing process that you notice. Once you have created the list, sit mindfully with full body awareness and notice what you feel in your body. Do particular sensations come up for you? Observe where they are in your body. Pendulate and Titrate these sensations. Refer back to the section on somatic experiencing if you need to refresh your memory.

Write in your diary about your experience of doing this exercise.

DAY 29

Exercise 21: Visualising the Kind of Person that You Need to Be to Overcome Your Blocks.

This is a new exercise. Set this up in the same way as your other visualisations. Knowing the steps that you need to take forward for greater healing, what kind of person do you need to be able to do that? Visualise yourself as that person. What qualities do you need? What skill set? What do you look like? What is the environment like around you?

After the visualisation, write in your diary what you discovered about yourself. Draw a picture of yourself as that person.

DAY 30

Exercise 22: Finding Support for Yourself.

This is a new exercise. Today, take concrete steps to reach out and find the kind of support you need to ensure that your healing work continues to move forward. Make a plan as to what you are going to do next to enable you to carry on healing. Reflect upon what has been helpful for you so far in this journey. What needs strengthening in what you have done? What is the kind of help that you feel you need at this point? Draw a mind map of where you are at now. Or draw a picture.

DAY 31

Celebration!

Take the time today to really celebrate having got this far in your healing journey. Well done! You have worked really hard and you are able to heal.

CHAPTER 10

How do you know when you are fully healed?

What are the indicators that tell you that you have healed from the conditions that were troubling you, and how do you know when you are fully healed? These are important questions. When you are in the healing process, it is often difficult to tell if you are making progress because changes can often be very slow and subtle. Also, every person is unique and there is not a generalised external measure. For this reason, it is important for you to keep your own references and to have an idea of what the base line was for you, and what has changed along the way. This is the purpose of the journal and activation chart; to enable you to see whether the things that would previously trigger you, still trigger you now. What you are looking for, is less reactivity and sensitivity to triggers, and also a lessening of fear and anxiety, or anger. An overall diminishment of the difficult, uncomfortable feelings. At the same time witnessing yourself being more open, less fearful; more ready to try new things. A greater feeling of happiness; feeling more comfortable, and less pain. When you look at your window of tolerance, are you able to stay within it more of the time?

The other indicator of increasing wellness, is that you no longer identify with 'your story'. You see and experience a life outside of that story. Are you able to stop identifying with the story of what went wrong in your life? Are you able to not be in the pain and limitation of it anymore? Can you know that the story is there, but that it no longer defines you? It was an important experience, but it doesn't run your life. Wisdom and strength can be gleaned from it; and it need not prevent you from being happy now.

When we are traumatised, we get stuck with memories that keep replaying in the present moment, making us believe that 'that thing' is still happening. But when you heal, those memories change so that they are now something that you can talk about, but they no longer have any power to trigger you. There is no longer any activation or 'charge' with the memories. You can talk about them in the form of a story.

So, when assessing if you have healed, how much of the above has changed for you? Spend some time looking back over your diary and activation chart, thinking about your window of tolerance and notice what is different now. I am sure that you will find a difference. Sometimes it feels like there has been no improvement when you are focussing on one thing, but if you explore more widely, you will see that other things have changed. We cannot know what has to change first before the thing that was the main difficulty to you changes. So, be mindful to the small and subtle changes.

Another thing that can happen is that your life experiences can spiral. For instance, you feel like you have healed a lot then suddenly find yourself in a bad situation again. However, if you look deeply, it is not bad in the way that it was before. Your life has gone in a spiral and it feels like you are back at the starting point but it is an upward spiral and you have returned to a similar position but higher up, and this time around you have handled the situation with more wisdom than before. You will most likely also move through and out of it more quickly. It is important not to feel despair or to plummet again when you find yourself back in those places. Instead, see it as an opportunity to practise more more compassion for yourself and others. We are human. Being human means that we can suffer. It also means that we-have an amazing capacity to transcend that suffering; and when we do transcend it, we have an incredible capacity to grow, to transform, and to attain remarkable wisdom so that we now become a force of light and goodness that lifts the hearts of others who are suffering.

If you find yourself at a place where you hear yourself saying.... *'nothing has changed'*, don't believe it. You will certainly have changed. You cannot go backwards. You are learning and gaining new insight all the time. Your brain is growing and becoming more integrated, giving you greater capacity for more growth. Most importantly, your soul is gaining more wisdom and becoming more luminous. So be prepared, these times may happen when you feel despondent that you have 'done all this work' and you are back at the same point. Don't allow yourself to feel a disappointment and a feeling of setback.

One of my biggest feelings of setback was when I had finally got out of a difficult marriage and spent several years healing. I thought *'Yeah, my life is finally on track'*. I then met another partner who I thought was the love of my life, and everything was going to be happy and smooth from this point on. What I didn't realise was that there were still some very big patterns that I had not healed. The earlier work that I had done had given me a degree of consciousness and awareness, which was preparing me for this big experience. The new partner turned out very differently from the previous one, but the marriage brought with it some very big and difficult challenges which revealed a deeper, underlying pattern and commonality between this relationship and previous relationships. It showed me the deep patterns of pain I had through attachment damage that had happened as a baby. So now I was on an epic journey to heal that damage. I tried to do things differently in this new marriage, but still I could not sustain it because there was too much trauma both within my husband and myself, so, eventually, we had to part. It was an enormous period of pain and learning, but also a-profound healing — not only for myself, but my whole family. It was this experience that finally launched me on the path to becoming a trauma therapist and teacher. It taught me humility, compassion, and perseverance, and — most importantly — how to love myself, rather than feel shame because I had 'failed', again, to love someone else.

Please never give up on yourself. Be there for youself, and keep going no matter what happens. I believe in you, and I know that you can do it. Be kind, be gentle, and love yourself.

Personal responsibility and Creativity

Another indicator of whether you are getting well, is when you stop making others responsible for what is wrong in your life. You let go of blaming them, or feeling that they have got to change before you can be happy. Begin to take responsibility for yourself. Only you can change you. This means that even when people appear to be doing bad things that hurt you, you still have the power to decide if you are going to stay with hurt, or whether you are going to move away from it. Perhaps you can stop taking what others are doing as a personal attack or affront on you. Remember that we create a lens through which we are continually interpreting the actions and words of others. Our early experiences create a belief system and a lens through which we view the world.

If you find yourself with 'stuck statements' such as *"there is no love"* or *"this always happens to me"* or *"you can't trust men/women"*, then you can suspect that these thoughts are not true and that they are going to keep you trapped. They are the replaying of old experiences that are still shaping your life and your decision-making, causing you to make bad choices, and blaming others for them. Choose to take responsibility for whatever shows up in your life. Know that you are powerful, and that you CREATE EVERYTHING. It wouldn't show up if you were not the author of it in some way. So, be mindful, and explore in what way you were part of what has just happened to you. In what way did you lend the shape and tone to this experience. When you choose to take responsibility, you will find that you have tremendous power and your healing can happen much more quickly.

In the book 'Seth Speaks' The Eternal Validity of the Soul by Jane Roberts personal responsibility and creativity are explored in the much broader context of the evolution of the soul. As souls we have immense creative power and the purpose of our evolution is to use that creative power to grow in consciousness. We can use it to create whatever reality we choose. Consciousness grows as we understand that whatever circumstances we find ourselves in, it is because we have created them. Seth goes on to say:

"Illness and suffering are the results of the misdirection of creative energy, they are (as much) a part of the creative force, than say, health and vitality. Suffering is not good for the soul, unless it teaches you how to stop suffering.....

It is possible to have sane and healthy minds, within healthy bodies, to have a sane planet"

We are not meant to suffer. If you hold the belief that humans are born to suffer, then set it aside. Our role is to create beauty, harmony, health, abundance and to grow in our capacity to expand this throughout the universe. Illness, and destruction are choices of the way that we use the creative energy that is available to us.

Let's Pause and Look back at what has changed

The rewards that you reap in your own health and well being and the healing of your trauma, are in direct proportion to the effort that you put into this creative process.

We have gone through, in this book, the most important fundamental areas of healing. It is a step along the way of achieving even greater health and well being. The journey doesn't end but each step brings you closer to your goal.

One important achievement if you have faithfully followed through the process to this point, is that you will have developed a greater capacity for self reflection and the ability to direct your energy towards outcomes that support you.

Take some time NOW for reflection. Set a time to get out your diary and charts and search back to when you started this phase of your healing. As you ask yourself the following questions, compare then and now, and write about it in your diary.

1. What was my over-riding symptom then? How bad was it on a scale of 1 -10 (with 1 not very bad, and 10 really serious)? Do I still have that symptom now? Have I found a better way to be with it? Is it as frequent?

2. What are my sleep patterns like now? Better, worse, or the same?

3. What are my eating habits like now? Have they improved?

4. What is my overall physical health like now?

5. What is my exercise routine? How has that changed?

6. How am I getting on in my relationships? Where have I improved? Where do I find greater ease?

7. What is my concentration and focus like now? Rate it 1 - 10.

8. What is my sense of purpose like now? Am I more engaged in my life?

9. How quickly do I recover from upsets now? Is it easier?

10. How do I manage now when I get triggered? Am I still as reactive?

11. What is my self-care like now? Do I take better care than previously?

12. Has anything changed in my hearing and sight? (One client I had could see and hear better after doing this work).

13. What is my libido like now?

14. What is my self-talk like now? Am I kinder and more compassionate to myself?

15. What are my thinking patterns like now? Do I have negative thoughts spiraling endlessly in my head or is there greater peace?

16. How much am I caught up in the past now, and how much can I be in the present moment?

17. What are my levels of optimism and positive thinking like now? Am I able to put a positive spin on a situation where previously I had felt that it was all bad and hopeless?

18. What is my capacity to feel self-compassion?

19. How much do I blame and judge other people now, and project my pain onto others?

20. How much do I think that I have to be responsible for other people's lives now, rather than trusting that they can take care of themselves?

21. What is my relationship like with myself now? Am I more caring, supportive, and loving? Am I prepared to put myself first, and make sure that I am well before I dive in to looking after others?

Are there any other questions relevant to you? If so, then reflect on them and rate them as above.

After you have looked at each of those points, think about what you need to do to improve each of them. Where is there room for improvement? Don't be over zealous. Look for small, gradual changes that you can make for yourself in a really kind way. Small, kind changes are more likely to stick than big plans that fall by the wayside.

Above all, your focus should always be on self-care and love.

Write all your insights and evaluations down, and then sum it up with a statement, such as: *"Today, I find that I have made (this kind of a change) in these (areas) and I am doing well with my healing work. I commit to continue to grow and I plan to implement these following changes… (list the changes that you will make)."* Work out a schedule for bringing these new changes into your life. Now schedule a time when you will do your next review.

Read this all aloud to yourself

Do you have a friend with whom you can share your progress? If so, schedule a time to be able to talk about what you have discovered with them.

Well done! Now go out and celebrate with some nice activity. You deserve it!

Therapy approaches for Trauma Healing - Don't do this alone - you need help:

Healing is very hard to do alone, especially when healing from trauma. It is important to find support. You may need to change your friends if you are surrounded by negative people that don't understand what you are going through, or at least to find some new ones. If you can begin to join some activities that are resourcing — such as yoga, dancing, theatre performance, or other beneficial activities — you may make new friends in those places. You can also look online for trauma-healing forums or groups, and join in with some conversations there. It is important to know that you are not alone, and that what you are going through is similar to many other people that have had difficult experiences. We all have the same kind of nervous system and body, and there is a certain commonality between what we all experience. Having friends who are understanding and supportive is really helpful when you are going through difficult and challenging situations.

Another important and helpful thing to do is to find a good therapist who understands trauma healing, and to book yourself some sessions.   Don't just go for straight psychotherapy; just talking about what happened in childhood without integrating it through the body, can be re-traumatising. If you choose psychotherapy, choose a form which is body centred – one that will help you get in touch with what you are holding in your body. There are various approaches to healing trauma, and different therapy forms.

How to take your Healing further - More Resources

Below, are some approaches that you can explore and see what is available in your area.

Somatic Experiencing

This is the work created by Dr Peter Levine. You will find that there are probably some somatic experiencing therapists in your area. This is particularly useful if you have had an accident or short-term difficult experience. I have already introduced you to some somatic experiencing approaches - with titration and pendulation as approaches to discover how you are embodying and holding frozen trauma energies in your body. Finding a good therapist with these skills will really help the work that you are already doing.

EMDR

This form of therapy was discovered by a psychologist, Francine Shapiro, in the 1980s. It stands for Eye Movement Desensitisation Repatterning. It works with how memories are stored in the brain, and how we can change the memories by talking about the experience whilst at the same time giving the body bi-lateral stimulation. This could be sensory, auditory or visual.

Dr Bessel van der Kolk, trauma expert, initially thought that this was a really silly therapy because it involves 'waggling fingers' in front of the client's eyes and getting them to follow the movement of the fingers. However, he was eventually persuaded to try it, and found that it was very successful.

He has since adopted it in his own clinic, and is particularly impressed with how it helps with single episode acute trauma. And, although it can be helpful in more complex trauma, it is not so useful for developmental trauma, where there are difficult attachment and attunement issues to be healed.

Internal Family Systems Therapy

This therapy was created by Richard Schwartz. He developed it whilst working with very highly traumatised exiles. It is regarded as being very effective for more complex forms of trauma.

In Internal Family Systems therapy (IFS), an individual's consciousness is considered to be composed of a central self with three types of sub-personalities or parts. These are named as 'managers', 'exiles', and 'firefighters'. Each individual part has its own perspective, interests, memories, and viewpoint. A core tenet of IFS is that every part has a positive intent for you, even if its actions or effects are counterproductive, or cause dysfunction. This means that there is never any reason to fight with, coerce, or try to eliminate a part; the IFS method promotes internal connection and harmony. In this therapy, the therapist will encourage you to get to know the different parts that are within you, and help you to discover what their roles are. You will then be encouraged to allow each part to have a voice and to begin to talk to the other parts. The aim is for the parts to come into an agreement as to what is the best, most integrative approach for you to be able to heal.

Sensorimotor Psychotherapy

This therapy approach was pioneered by Dr Pat Ogden. In the 1970s, she recognised that many of her patients treated with normal psychotherapy approaches were simply reliving the past without making any progress. Simply talking about negative experiences was causing clients to become triggered into traumatic activations. She recognised the link between the body and psychological issues, and created Sensorimotor Psychotherapy which is a blending together of somatic therapy and psychotherapy. This therapeutic approach is a whole-body system where posture, movement, and sensation are all part of the information system that is accessed in the healing process. Helping clients to tune into the unspoken messages in a body posture for instance, can help to release the emotional, psychological, and physical pain held in the body.

Family Constellations Therapy

Family Constellations Therapy was created by Bert Hellinger. However, he has preferred not to describe this process as a therapy or to define a theory behind it. A constellation is a group participatory event. The group is lead by the person who is making the enquiry about an area of healing that is needed. Each group member is then allocated to play a different role in the story that causes the suffering.

The focus of the constellation is to transform inter-generational trauma caused by experiences, which may have been unspoken or hidden, that happened in early generations, and the burden of which have been passed down the family line. This could be such things as murder, child abuse, loss, shame. Future generations have had to carry the unresolved issues of previous generations, and this may show up as trauma in you as an individual in your life.

Bert Hellinger prefers to define the core aspects of the work as balance, belonging, and order. These principles guide the facilitator of a family constellation session. They work without judgement and with acceptance for 'what is'.

Whatever experience comes up in the group will be considered to be informative and releasing of the carried burden. It is rather like a pyscho-drama played out between the participants that will bring a sense of knowing and release of the suffering of the person who the constellation is for.

Neuro Affective Relational Model (NARM)

Developed by Laurence Heller, this is a cutting-edge approach for complex trauma. It particularly addresses attachment, relational, and developmental trauma. It explores the identity of who we truly are underneath the patterned responses of relating to ourselves and others. It works on psychological issues by learning self-regulation of the nervous system through body awareness.

"Humans suffer from an endless number of emotional problems and challenges, most of these can be traced to early developmental and shock trauma that compromise the development of one or more of the five core capacities."

Laurence Heller

Biodynamic Craniosacral Therapy

There are a number of different approaches to craniosacral therapy and some are called cranio osteopathy. It is, particularly, the bio-dynamic craniosacral therapy as developed by Dr Franklyn Sills that gives a deep holding and awareness of trauma. This is a hands on, body-work based therapy which also works with psychological, emotional, and spiritual experiences held in the body.

Neuro Feedback:

Also called neuro-therapy or neurobiofeedback, this is a type of biofeedback that uses real time displays of brain activity (using a computer screen) to teach self-regulation of brain function. Sensors are placed on the scalp to measure electrical activity. A computer game can be played which rewards good self-regulation of brain activity.

Limbic System Therapy

This is a therapy approach created by Dr Bessel van der Kolk; a researcher, psychotherapist, and long-time pioneer in the field of trauma healing. He has highlighted the importance of working with the limbic system, which is a set of structures in the brain that regulate autonomic or endocrine function in response to emotional stimuli such as anger, happiness, and fear as well as memories. As you have read previously, these are all important parts of healing trauma, so, by being aware of how all this is processed in the brain is helpful in healing even complex PTSD.

Finding a therapist skilled in trauma healing who can work with a number of different approaches

Above, I have described some of the main therapeutic approaches for healing trauma. Depending on the nature of your trauma, some might be more appropriate than others. It is also important to feel comfortable with your chosen therapist. You need to feel safe, and that they are there to support and help you. They need to have empathy and understanding, as well as really good boundaries. You may find a therapist who has a variety of therapy healing skills.

In addition to therapy work, other activities, previously described, are helpful for healing trauma — especially those involving movement, body awareness, and interacting with other people.

Healing Waters Sanctuary

We also offer trauma healing at Healing Waters Sanctuary, which is where I offer my therapy work and teaching. You can find us through the website: www.healing-waters.co.uk

Or through my personal website which is: julietyelverton.com

Trauma Healing Videos

I have also created a range of trauma healing videos which you can sign up for by going to my website. They come daily via an email, and encourage you to do the trauma healing somatic exercises on a daily basis. They do not in themselves replace working with a therapist, but together with this book, they can still help you significantly. It really depends upon how deep and complex your difficulty is. But do check them out, they are a small investment and will support the other work that you are doing.

Wow you have made it this far!

Congratulations on making it almost to the end of the book. If you have skipped over sections to get here, then that is still great. There are lots of different parts to this book, and some may be appropriate to you now and some may be more appropriate later. There are lots of goals in it to pursue and to achieve. Each one is a building block towards healing trauma. Only you know the best way to put it all together. You can flip backwards and forwards through this book and do the exercises that you find effective, many times. Then, when you are ready for it, you can move onto another part. If your healing journey is spiraling around, and you sometimes feel lost, then you can go back to earlier parts. You will also find that, as you return to parts, you will have new experiences. The important thing, is to not overwhelm yourself, and to keep celebrating each small victory as you learn to be kinder and more compassionate towards yourself.

This book, although it has a lot of content, is an introduction to trauma healing. Consider that as you heal your personal trauma, that it is one strand in a web of your family trauma, which is a result of your generational trauma and collective trauma of the planet. In healing yourself, you have dramatically strengthened the strand in this web. Everyone around you will have greater capacity to heal as a result of the work that you have done here.

Personally you will have much more energy as a result of doing this. Should you feel inspired, you can share this with others. If you are able to just open one other person's awareness to the necessity of healing their trauma, then the world can change. It's important to think:

"it has to stop with me. I am not going to pass this trauma on to my children, family or friends".

If you want to increase your understanding of trauma healing, below is a list of titles and important research that can help you go deeper. You will also find that these same people have plenty of content on YouTube (videos or podcasts), or that you can get their books as audio books. I invite you to do this.

BIBLIOGRAPHY

Trauma Healing Researchers and Authors:

1. Dr Bessel van der Kolk.

Bessel van der Kolk, MD has spent his career studying how children and adults adapt to traumatic experiences, and has translated emerging findings from neuroscience and attachment research to develop and study a range of potentially effective treatments for traumatic stress in children and adults.

He says: *"Being able to feel safe with other people is probably the single most important aspect of mental health; safe connections are fundamental to meaningful and satisfying lives."*

"Neuroscience research shows that the only way we can change the way we feel is by becoming aware of our inner experience and learning to befriend what is going on inside ourselves."

His books:

The Body Keeps the Score.

Numerous research papers

Videos and Talks on YouTube and Internet

2. Dr Peter Levine

Dr Peter A. Levine received his PhD in medical biophysics from the University of California in Berkeley, and also holds a doctorate in psychology from International University. He has worked in the field of stress and trauma for over 40 years, and is the developer of the Somatic Experiencing method. Peter's original contribution to the field of Body-

Psychotherapy was honoured in 2010 when he received the Lifetime Achievement award from United States Association for Body Psychotherapy (USABP)

His books:

Waking the Tiger

In an Unspoken Voice

Trauma Proofing your Kids (co-authored)

Sexual Healing

Trauma Through a Child's Eyes (co-authored)

Trauma and Memory - Brain & Body in a Search for the Past

Numerous talks and videos on YouTube and the internet

3. Dr Pat Ogden:

Pat Ogden founded the Sensorimotor Psychotherapy Institute, located in Boulder, Colorado. She is the Director of the institute, which focuses on educating and training clinicians in sensorimotor therapy techniques used to address developmental, attachment, and trauma issues. Her 2006 book, *Trauma and the Body: A Sensorimotor Approach to Psychotherapy*, outlines her approach.

Ogden works as a trainer, consultant, and clinician, applying her psychotherapeutic and somatic techniques to various groups of people, including prisoners, trauma victims, and psychiatric patients. Ogden is also the co-founder of the Hakomi Institute with Ron Kurtz.

Her Books:

Trauma and the Body - A Sensorimotor Approach. - Co-authored with Pat Ogden, Kekuni Minton and Clare Pain

Wisdom of the Body

Dr Gabor Mate:

Gabor Maté CM, is a Hungarian-born Canadian physician, with a background in family practice and a special interest in childhood development and trauma, and in their potential lifelong impacts on physical and mental health, including on autoimmune disease, cancer, ADHD, addictions, and a wide range of other conditions.

His Books:

Hang Onto Your Kids

When the Body Says No

In the Realm of Hungry Ghosts

ADD

Dr Babette Rothschild:

Babette Rothschild, MSW, has been a practitioner since 1976 and a teacher and trainer since 1992. She is a bestselling author of six books, all published by WW Norton and translated into more than a dozen languages.

Her Books:

The Body Remembers

8 Keys to Safe Trauma Recovery

Trauma Essentials

Babette Rothschild Chart of Arousal states.

AUTONOMIC NERVOUS SYSTEM: PRECISION REGULATION
** WHAT TO LOOK FOR **

	LETHARGIC Parasympathetic I (PNS I)	CALM Parasympathetic II (PNS II) Ventral Vagus	ACTIVE/ALERT Sympathetic I (SNS I)	FLIGHT/FIGHT Sympathetic II (SNS II)	HYPER FREEZE Sympathetic III (SNS III)	HYPO FREEZE Parasympathetic III (PNS III) Dorsal Vagus Collapse
		"Normal" Life →	←		Threat to Life ← →	
PRIMARY STATE	Apathy, Depression	Safe, Clear Thinking, Social Engagement	Alert, Ready to Act	React to Danger	Await Opportunity to Escape	Prepare for Death
AROUSAL	Too Low	Low	Moderate	High	Extreme Overload	Excessive Overwhelm Induces Hypoarousal
MUSCLES	Slack	Relaxed/toned	Toned	Tense	Rigid (deer in the headlights)	Flaccid
RESPIRATION	Shallow	Easy, often into belly	Increasing rate	Fast, often in upper chest	Hyperventilation	Hypo-ventilation
HEART RATE	Slow	Resting	Quicker or more forceful	Quick and/or forceful	Tachycardia (very fast)	Bradycardia (very slow)
BLOOD PRESSURE	Likely low	Normal	On the rise	Elevated	Significantly high	Significantly low
PUPILS, EYES, EYE LIDS	Pupils smaller, lids may be heavy	Pupils smaller, eyes moist, eye lids relaxed	Pupils widening, eyes less moist, eye lids toned	Pupils very dilated, eyes dry, eye lids tensed/raised	Pupils very small or dilated, eyes very dry, lids very tense	Lids drooping, eyes closed or open and fixed
SKIN TONE	Variable	Rosy hue, despite skin color (blood flows to skin)	Less rosy hue, despite skin color (blood flows to skin)	Pale hue, despite skin color (blood flow to muscles)	May be pale and/or flushed	Noticeably pale
HUMIDITY — Skin	Dry	Dry	Increased sweat	Increased sweat, may be cold	Cold sweat	Cold sweat
HUMIDITY — Mouth	Variable	Moist	Less moist	Dry	Dry	Dry
HANDS & FEET (TEMPERATURE)	May be warm or cool	Warm	Cool	Cold	Extremes of cold & hot	Cold
DIGESTION	Variable	Increase	Decrease	Stops	Evacuate bowel & bladder	Stopped
EMOTIONS (LIKELY)	Grief, sadness, shame, disgust	Calm, pleasure, love, sexual arousal	Anger, shame, disgust, anxiety, excitement, sexual climax	Rage, fear	Terror, may be dissociation	May be too dissociated to feel anything
CONTACT WITH SELF & OTHERS	Withdrawn	Should be accessible	Possible	Limited	Not likely	Impossible
FRONTAL CORTEX	May or may not be accessible	Probable	Should be accessible	May or may not be accessible	Likely inaccessible	Inaccessible
INTEGRATION	Not likely	Likely	Likely	Not likely	Impossible	Impossible
RECOMMENDED INTERVENTION	Activate, Gently Increase Energy	Continue Therapy Direction	Continue Therapy Direction	Put on Brakes	Slam on Brakes	Medical Emergency CALL PARAMEDICS

*Observe client states: To modulate arousal with brakes. Adjust in yourself: To think clearly & prevent vicarious trauma & compassion fatigue.

© 2000, 2014, 2016 Babette Rothschild Sources: Multiple medical & physiology texts; P.Levine 2010: S.Porges, 2011
Reprinted with permission from *The Body Remembers, Volume 2: Revolutionizing Trauma Treatment* (W.W. Norton, 2017)

This table is also available as a laminated Card (ISBN 978-0-393-71280-3) and Wall Poster (ISBN 978-0-393-71281-0). To order, call 800-233-4830 or visit www.norton.com.

Laurence Heller:

Dr Laurence Heller, after a long career as a therapist (he co-founded the Gestalt Institute of Denver in 1972, followed by the Rocky Mountain Psychotherapy Institute), developed a therapeutic model that integrates psychotherapy with Somatic Experiencing (SE), called The NeuroAffective Relational Model™ or NARM

His Books:

Healing Developmental Trauma

Crash Course - Healing Auto Accident. Trauma and Recovery- Co authored

Karlton Terry

Pre and Perinatal educator

Karlton Terry IPPE Certified Principal Teacher Cofounder IPPE - Institute for Pre and Perinatal Education.

His Books:

Sperm Journey/Egg Journey

Pre- and Peri-natal Trauma (PPI)

Institutions:

Karuna Institute - Established by Franklyn and Maura Sills.

Somatic Experiencing Institute - Established by Dr Peter Levine.

IPPE - Institute for Pre and Perinatal Education. - Co founded by Karlton Terry

POST SCRIPT

A final Note From Juliet

Gratitude

I hold gratitude and thanks for all my friends and family and to all those that have believed in me. Not only that, but I have gratitude for all the challenges in my life, especially those painful and uncomfortable experiences. There are many that were hard to endure but through that process of extreme stress and pressure I have found the means within myself to transform them and bring forth this book. My prayer is that you are helped by it and that you yourself will know that there is always an unseen hand supporting you and guiding you forward. You are a being of infinite light, a part of the divine and that you have the ability to create the life that you desire.

Summary

This is by no means an exhaustive list of all the possible help that is available in the world today. There is an enormous amount of research happening, and many approaches to healing trauma. As Dr Pat Ogden says, *"there is no one way"*. Each person is different. But what is unanimously agreed is that in order to heal trauma, it is necessary to create a sense of safety. Healing Trauma is about calming down the primitive brain and updating the memory to the present moment. Anything that helps you to engage in an experience of well-being and connection in the 'here and now' is going to be helpful to you.

If you would like to contact me and get any support, please email me at juliet@healing-waters.co.uk and I will do what I can to be of service to you.

Be well, Be Happy and remember that you hold the means to your recovery within yourself.

Juliet Yelverton

Remember if you want to begin working now, in a guided way, scan this QR code and you can check out my 'How To Heal Your Trauma' online programme.

And finally I leave you with some informative infographics from NICABM and this wisdom from the Dalai Lama.

Time is always moving on; nothing can stop it. We **can't** change the past, but we can shape the future. The more compassionate you are, the more you will find inner peace

How Trauma Can Affect Your Window of Tolerance

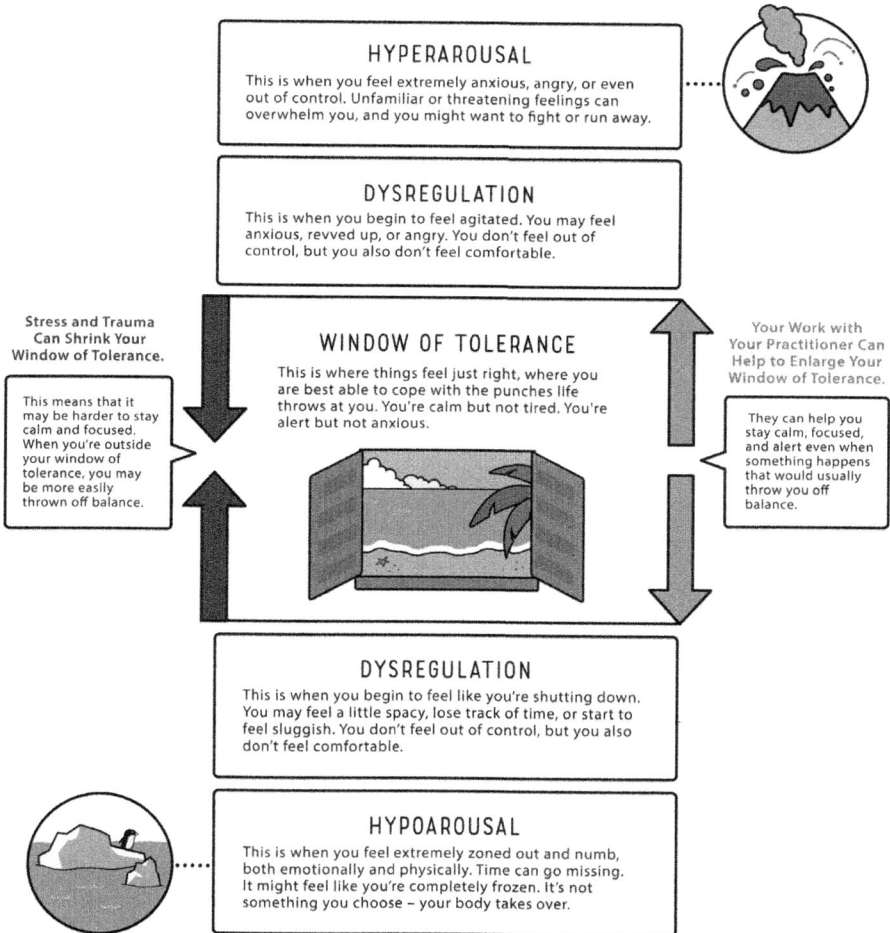

HYPERAROUSAL

This is when you feel extremely anxious, angry, or even out of control. Unfamiliar or threatening feelings can overwhelm you, and you might want to fight or run away.

DYSREGULATION

This is when you begin to feel agitated. You may feel anxious, revved up, or angry. You don't feel out of control, but you also don't feel comfortable.

Stress and Trauma Can Shrink Your Window of Tolerance.

This means that it may be harder to stay calm and focused. When you're outside your window of tolerance, you may be more easily thrown off balance.

WINDOW OF TOLERANCE

This is where things feel just right, where you are best able to cope with the punches life throws at you. You're calm but not tired. You're alert but not anxious.

Your Work with Your Practitioner Can Help to Enlarge Your Window of Tolerance.

They can help you stay calm, focused, and alert even when something happens that would usually throw you off balance.

DYSREGULATION

This is when you begin to feel like you're shutting down. You may feel a little spacy, lose track of time, or start to feel sluggish. You don't feel out of control, but you also don't feel comfortable.

HYPOAROUSAL

This is when you feel extremely zoned out and numb, both emotionally and physically. Time can go missing. It might feel like you're completely frozen. It's not something you choose – your body takes over.

nicabm
www.nicabm.com

GUILT vs SHAME

Guilt and shame are not the same. Understanding the differences between them can help us work through our negative self-judgments.

When we are better able to grasp the difference between healthy guilt, unhealthy guilt, and shame, we can begin to halt self-criticism and reject shame messages.

Guilt is often experienced when we act against our values. Shame, on the other hand, is a deeply-held belief about our unworthiness as a person.

Here's a way to visualize it:

	HELPFUL GUILT (HEALTHY)	UNHELPFUL GUILT (UNHEALTHY)	SHAME
DEFINITION	Helpful guilt is a feeling of psychological discomfort about something we've done that is objectively wrong.	Unhelpful guilt is a feeling of psychological discomfort about something we've done against our irrationally high standards.	Shame is an intensely painful feeling of being fundamentally flawed.
EXAMPLE	Chris hit someone while driving drunk and feels guilty.	Pat forgot a coworker's name and feels terribly guilty about it.	Jamie feels like a worthless person who is only taking up people's time and wasting space in the world.
CAUSE OF FEELING	Helpful guilt is caused by actions or behaviors that break objective definitions of right and wrong.	Unhelpful guilt is caused by actions or behaviors that break irrationally high standards.	Shame is caused by an innate sense of being worthless or inherently defective.
WHEN IT DEVELOPS	We can experience guilt as early as age 3-6. (Developmentally, guilt is a more mature emotion than shame.)	We can experience guilt as early as age 3-6.	We can experience shame as early as 15 months. (That's why shame is more deeply wired in our brain and is more difficult to reverse.)
WHY WE FEEL THIS	We act in a way that breaks objective standards of moral behavior.	We act in a way that breaks irrational standards of behavior developed early in childhood to please an adult.	We see ourselves as unworthy and deeply flawed.

nicabm
www.nicabm.com

GUILT vs SHAME

OUTCOME

Potentially positive.

Healthy guilt allows us to seek forgiveness and correct a wrong. It can lead to healing.

Negative.

Unhealthy guilt leads us to emphasize self-punishment over behavior change, trapping us in guilt.

Negative.

Shame causes us to fear that we will be rejected, so it tempts us to disconnect from others and avoid what causes us shame.

It could even start us down a path of deeper mental health problems like depression and substance abuse.

RESOLUTION

Healthy guilt resolves as we repair the damage we caused.

Unhealthy guilt remains until we correct irrational beliefs.

Shame is internalized and deeply connected to our sense of who we are which makes it more difficult to resolve.

HOW TO WORK WITH

Face the behavior that hurt self and others.

Take responsibility for the harm done.

Seek forgiveness from the person affected.

Change destructive behavior and attitudes that created the harm.

Reclaim wholeness and heal relationship with the person affected.

Separate and resolve healthy guilt to uncover unhealthy guilt.

Practice self-compassion and work to understand that everyone possesses a combination of strengths and weaknesses.

Seek connection with others. Joining a self-help group can offer support.

Exercise self-compassion to shift feelings of shame and move awareness away from self-criticism or proof of inadequacy.

Pursue relationships. Nurture connections and a sense of belonging with others.

HOW **ANGER** AFFECTS YOUR BRAIN AND BODY

1. The first spark of anger activates the amygdala before you're even aware of it.
2. The amygdala activates the hypothalamus.
3. The hypothalamus signals the pituitary gland by discharging corticotropin-releasing hormone (CRH).
4. The pituitary activates the adrenal glands by releasing adrenocorticotropic hormone (ACTH).
5. The adrenal glands secrete stress hormones like cortisol, adrenaline, and noradrenaline.

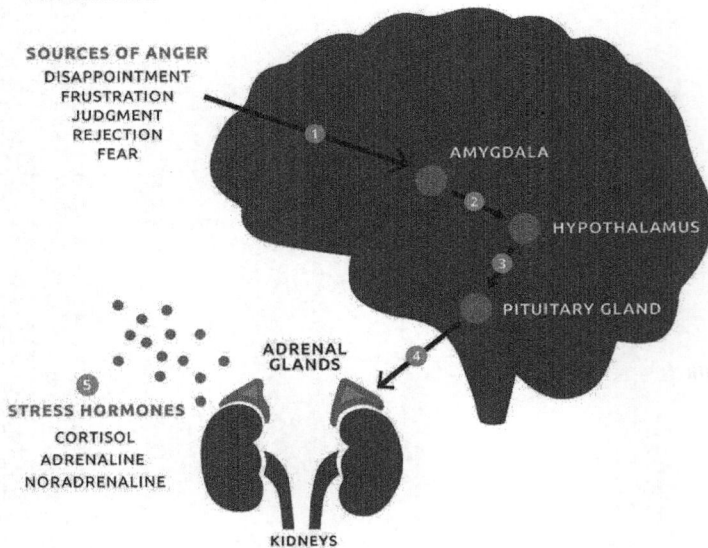

SOURCES OF ANGER
DISAPPOINTMENT
FRUSTRATION
JUDGMENT
REJECTION
FEAR

AMYGDALA

HYPOTHALAMUS

PITUITARY GLAND

ADRENAL GLANDS

STRESS HORMONES
CORTISOL
ADRENALINE
NORADRENALINE

KIDNEYS

nicabm
www.nicabm.com
© 2017 The National Institute for the Clinical Application of Behavioral Medicine

HOW **ANGER** AFFECTS YOUR BRAIN AND BODY

HOW ANGER CHANGES YOUR BRAIN

1. Elevated cortisol causes neurons to accept too much calcium through their membrane. A calcium overload can make cells fire too frequently and die. The hippocampus and prefrontal cortex (PFC) are particularly vulnerable to cortisol and these negative effects.

PREFRONTAL CORTEX

Elevated cortisol causes a loss of neurons in the prefrontal cortex (PCF). Suppressed activity in the PFC prevents you from using your best judgment - it keeps you from making good decisions and planning for the future.

HIPPOCAMPUS

Elevated cortisol kills neurons in the hippocampus and disrupts the creation of new ones. Suppressed activity in the hippocampus weakens short-term memory. It also prevents you from forming new memories properly. (This is why you might not remember what you want to say in an argument.)

2. Too much cortisol will decrease serotonin – that's the hormone that makes you happy. A decrease in serotonin can make you feel anger and pain more easily, as well as increase aggressive behavior and lead to depression.

HOW STRESS HORMONES AFFECT YOUR BODY

CARDIOVASCULAR SYSTEM
- Heart rate ↑
- Blood pressure ↑
- Arterial tension ↑
- Blood glucose level ↑
- Blood fatty acid level ↑

When these symptoms become chronic, blood vessels become clogged and damaged. This can lead to stroke and heart attack.

IMMUNE SYSTEM
- Thyroid function ↓
- The number of natural killer cells ↓
- The number of virus-infected cells ↑
- Incidence of cancer ↑

DIGESTIVE SYSTEM
- Blood flow ↓
- Metabolism ↓
- Dry mouth ↑

- Intraocular pressure ↑
- Eye sight ↓

- Migraines ↑
- Headaches ↑

- Bone density ↓

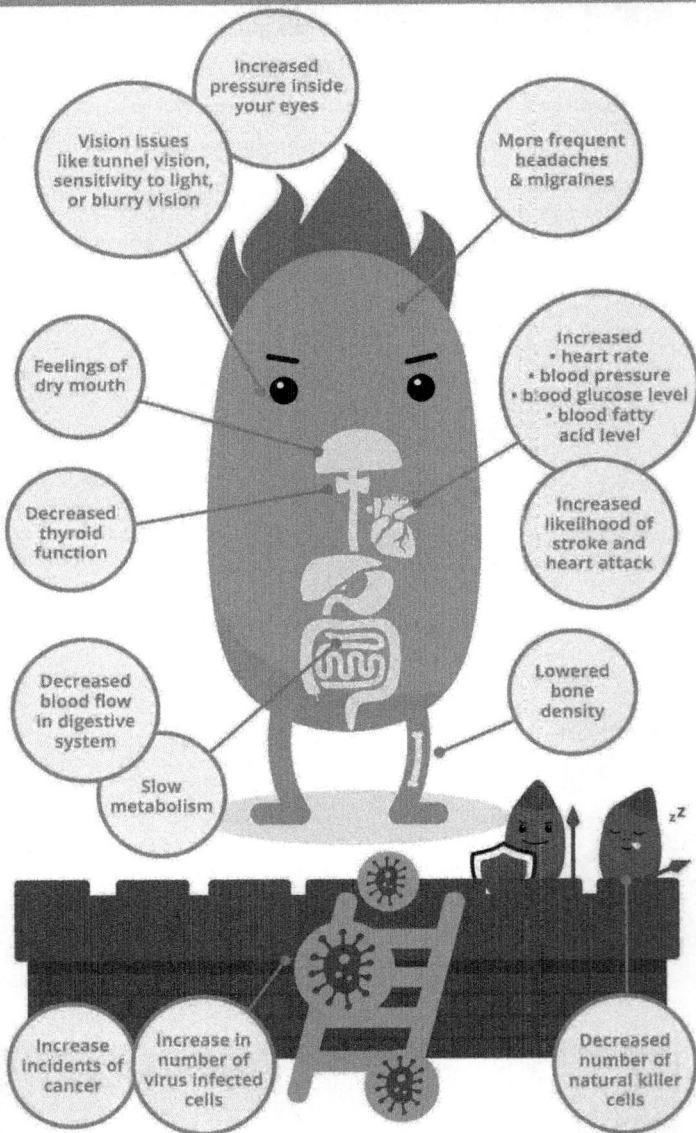

HOW ANGER AFFECTS YOUR BRAIN AND BODY: PART 3

Increased pressure inside your eyes

Vision issues like tunnel vision, sensitivity to light, or blurry vision

More frequent headaches & migraines

Feelings of dry mouth

Increased
• heart rate
• blood pressure
• blood glucose level
• blood fatty acid level

Decreased thyroid function

Increased likelihood of stroke and heart attack

Decreased blood flow in digestive system

Lowered bone density

Slow metabolism

Increase incidents of cancer

Increase in number of virus infected cells

Decreased number of natural killer cells

HOW A CAREGIVER'S TRAUMA CAN IMPACT A CHILD'S DEVELOPMENT

EARLY DEVELOPMENT

Caregiver With Traumatic Experience

Mother releases cortisol

Baby absorbs cortisol through placenta

Can impact baby's:
- HPA axis
- Central nervous system
- Limbic system
- Autonomic nervous system

Caregiver struggles to regulate

Attachment relationship between caregiver and child may be strained

Can impact child's:
- Development of a core sense of self
- Ability to integrate experiences
- Epigenetic expressions

ADULTHOOD

A Person Who Has Had a Caregiver With Untreated Trauma May:

Be more prone to PTSD after trauma

Struggle to repair after conflict

Struggle with relationships

Unintentionally bring out negative behaviors in others

Be emotionally detached

Be more prone to dissociate

BREAKING THE CYCLE OF TRAUMA

This can become a cycle, impacting future generations.

The good news is that healing trauma can break this loop. Seek help from a licensed health or mental health practitioner.

Parenting is a hard job, and this isn't meant to add to the stress of raising children. But it's critical to provide practitioners with information that can help them work more skillfully with patients who've experienced trauma and help them resolve their trauma. Trauma is not a life sentence – it's never too late to heal.

nicabm